CompTIA® Linux+™/LPIC-1
Portable Command Guide

All the commands for the CompTIA LX0-103 &
LX0-104 and LPI 101-400 & 102-400 exams
in one compact, portable resource

William "Bo" Rothwell

PEARSON IT
CERTIFICATION
800 East 96th Street
Indianapolis, Indiana 46240 USA

CompTIA® Linux+™/LPIC-1 Portable Command Guide

All the commands for the CompTIA LX0-103 & LX0-104 and LPI 101-400 & 102-400 exams in one compact, portable resource

William "Bo" Rothwell

Copyright © 2018 Pearson Education, Inc.

Published by:
Pearson IT Certification
800 East 96th Street
Indianapolis, IN 46240 USA

Printed in the United States of America

1   17

Library of Congress Control Number: 2017945102

ISBN-13: 978-0-7897-5711-1

ISBN-10: 0-7897-5711-7

Editor-in-Chief
Mark Taub

Product Line Manager
Brett Bartow

Executive Editor
Mary Beth Ray

Managing Editor
Sandra Schroeder

Development Editor
Christopher Cleveland

Project Editor
Mandie Frank

Copy Editor
Bart Reed

Technical Editor
Casey Boyles

Editorial Assistant
Vanessa Evans

Designer
Chuti Prasertsith

Composition
codeMantra

Indexer
Erika Millen

Proofreader
Larry Sulky

Warning and Disclaimer

Trademark Acknowledgments

Special Sales

For information about buying this title in bulk quantities, or for special sales opportunities (which may include electronic versions; custom cover designs; and content particular to your business, training goals, marketing focus, or branding interests), please contact our corporate sales department at corpsales@pearsoned.com or (800) 382-3419.

For government sales inquiries, please contact governmentsales@pearsoned.com.

For questions about sales outside the U.S., please contact intlcs@pearson.com.

Contents at a Glance

Contents

Part III: GNU and Unix Commands

Part V: Shell Scripting and Data Management

About the Author

At the impressionable age of 14, **William "Bo" Rothwell** crossed paths with a TRS-80 Micro Computer System (affectionately known as a "Trash 80"). Soon thereafter, the adults responsible for Bo made the mistake of leaving him alone with the TRS-80. He immediately dismantled it and held his first computer class, showing his friends what made this "computer thing" work.

Since this experience, Bo's passion for understanding how computers work and sharing this knowledge with others has resulted in a rewarding career in IT training. His experience includes Linux, Unix, IT security, Devops, and programming languages such as Perl, Python, Tcl, and BASH. He is the founder and lead instructor of One Course Source, an IT training organization.

About the Technical Reviewer

Casey Boyles started working in the IT field more than 25 years ago and quickly moved on to distributed application and database development. Casey later moved on to technical training and course development, where he specializes in full stack internet application development, database architecture, and systems security. Casey typically spends his time smoking cigars while "reading stuff and writing stuff."

Dedications

I have come to realize that I continuously put a large number of complex projects on my plate. To complete them all, I would either need to be a hermit or have a very understanding and supportive family. I am not a hermit.

Thank you Sarah, Julia, Mom, and Dad for your encouragement of my aspirations and willingness to accept my ludicrous, self-imposed workload.

Acknowledgments

If this book was solely the result of my efforts, then you should realize it wouldn't be close to half as good as it is now. My name gets to go on the cover, but this book, as with all that I write, is the result of a team effort.

Casey Boyles: Thank you for taking the role of Technical Reviewer! Your insights were very helpful.

Chris Cleveland: Thank you for keeping your finger on the pulse of this project. Someone needs to keep me in line!

Mary Beth Ray: Thank you again for providing me the opportunity to write another book.

We Want to Hear from You!

As the reader of this book, you are our most important critic and commentator. We value your opinion and want to know what we're doing right, what we could do better, what areas you'd like to see us publish in, and any other words of wisdom you're willing to pass our way.

We welcome your comments. You can email or write to let us know what you did or didn't like about this book—as well as what we can do to make our books better.

Please note that we cannot help you with technical problems related to the topic of this book.

When you write, please be sure to include this book's title and author as well as your name and email address. We will carefully review your comments and share them with the author and editors who worked on the book.

Email: feedback@pearsonitcertification.com

Mail: Pearson IT Certification
          ATTN: Reader Feedback
          800 East 96th Street
          Indianapolis, IN 46240 USA

Reader Services

Register your copy of *CompTIA Linux+/LPIC-1 Portable Command Guide* at www.pearsonitcertification.com for convenient access to downloads, updates, and corrections as they become available. To start the registration process, go to www.pearsonitcertification.com/register and log in or create an account*. Enter the product ISBN 9780789757111 and click Submit. When the process is complete, you will find any available bonus content under Registered Products.

*Be sure to check the box that you would like to hear from us to receive exclusive discounts on future editions of this product.

Command Syntax Conventions

The conventions used to present command syntax in this book are as follows:

- **Boldface** indicates commands and keywords that are entered literally as shown. In actual configuration examples and output (not general command syntax), boldface indicates commands that are manually input by the user (such as a **show** command).

- *Italic* indicates arguments for which you supply actual values.

- Vertical bars (|) separate alternative, mutually exclusive elements.

- Square brackets ([ ]) indicate an optional element.

- Braces ({ }) indicate a required choice.

- Braces within brackets ([{ }]) indicate a required choice within an optional element.

Introduction

I vividly recall, in my early days of working on Unix, heavily leaning on the knowledge provided by *UNIX in a Nutshell*. This publication was the right balance of simple documentation mixed with additional descriptions of the commands, files, and features of the Unix operating system.

In many ways, this book provides a similar experience—but with a twist. Unix and Linux have grown so large that a single "summary" book is no longer feasible. So, this book focuses specifically on the testable topics for the COMPTIA Linux+ and the LPIC Level 1 certification exams.

You might wonder how this book is different from a regular textbook or how it is different from standard Linux documentation (man or info pages). The best way to describe it is that it fits into the gap between these two. For each exam-testable topic, I provide a description and state the important options and features. Long, detailed descriptions are left for regular textbooks on this topic, and you won't find every single option, feature, variable, and configuration setting in this summary book—after all, how could we call it a "summary book" if we included all of that?

I hope you find this to be a reference source for you, both while preparing for the COMPTIA Linux+ or the LPIC Level 1 certification exam and while you are working in Linux after the exam.

Who Should Read This Book

This book is for those people preparing for the CompTIA Linux+ or the LPIC Level 1 certification exam, whether through self-study, on-the-job training and practice, or study via a training program. This book provides you with the depth of knowledge you need to pass these exams, as well as introduces valuable features of the Linux operating system.

Organization of This Book

Because this book is designed to help you prepare for the CompTIA Linux+ and the LPIC Level 1 certification exams, I have opted to match the organization of the book to align with the exam objective topics. There are 23 topics for the first exam, and those topics make up the first 23 chapters of this book. The last 20 chapters of this book match the exam objectives for the second exam. This organization should help aid you in your preparation for the exams.

Part I: System Architecture

- **Chapter 1, "Determine and Configure Hardware Settings"**—In this chapter, you are given an overview of the commands and files that provide you with information about hardware settings and the means to change these settings.

- **Chapter 2, "Boot the System"**—You learn how the system behaves during the boot process and how the administrator can modify this behavior in this chapter.

- **Chapter 3, "Change Runlevels / Boot Targets and Shut Down or Reboot System"**—In this chapter, you learn about runlevels and boot targets—two methods of modifying the state of the operating system.

Part II: Linux Installation and Package Management

- **Chapter 4, "Design Hard Disk Layout"**—In this chapter, you discover the essentials of how the hard disk structure affects the operating system.

- **Chapter 5, "Install a Boot Manager"**—In this chapter, you learn how to install the GRUB boot loader as well as learn about how to configure boot managers.

- **Chapter 6, "Manage Shared Libraries"**—This chapter focuses on how applications make use of shared libraries.

- **Chapter 7, "Use Debian Package Management"**—You learn in this chapter how to manage software packages on distributions that use the Debian package management system.

- **Chapter 8, "Use RPM and YUM Package Management"**—You learn in this chapter how to manage software packages on distributions that use the RPM package management system.

Part III: GNU and Unix Commands

- **Chapter 9, "Work on the Command Line"**—This chapter focuses on how to execute commands on the command line in Linux.

- **Chapter 10, "Process Text Streams Using Filters"**—In this chapter, you learn about filtering data using commands such as **grep**, **sed**, **cut**, **head**, and **tail**.

- **Chapter 11, "Perform Basic File Management"**—In this chapter, you learn how to manage files and directories using command-line tools.

- **Chapter 12, "Use Streams, Pipes, and Redirects"**—You learn in this chapter how to take the output of a command and send it to a file or another command.

- **Chapter 13, "Create, Monitor, and Kill Processes"**—You discover how to start and control processes in this chapter.

- **Chapter 14, "Modify Process Execution Priorities"**—This chapter focuses on managing how processes interact with the CPU.

- **Chapter 15, "Search Text Files Using Regular Expressions"**—Regular expressions, which provide the ability to use special characters to match strings, are covered in this chapter.

- **Chapter 16, "Perform Basic File Editing Operations Using vi"**—The always-available and ever-consistent vi editor is covered in this chapter.

Part IV: Devices, Linux Filesystems, and the Filesystem Hierarchy Standard

- **Chapter 17, "Create Partitions and Filesystems"**—You learn how to create partitions and filesystems using utilities such as **fdisk** and **mkfs** in this chapter.

- **Chapter 18, "Maintain the Integrity of Filesystems"**— In this chapter, you learn how to fix filesystem issues.

- **Chapter 19, "Control Mounting and Unmounting of Filesystems"**—You learn in this chapter how to make a filesystem available to the operating system using the mount technique.

- **Chapter 20, "Manage Disk Quotas"**—Discover how to manage how much disk space each user or group can use in this chapter.

- **Chapter 21, "Manage File Permissions and Ownership"**—In this chapter, you learn how to control access to files and directories using permissions.

- **Chapter 22, "Create and Change Hard and Symbolic Links"**—The focus of this chapter is managing file and directory links.

- **Chapter 23, "Find System Files and Place Files in the Correct Location"**—In this chapter, you learn how to find files by using commands such as the **find** command.

Part V: Shell Scripting and Data Management

- **Chapter 24, "Customize and Use the Shell Environment"**—Learn how to manage a user's shell environment by modifying customization files.

- **Chapter 25, "Customize or Write Simple Scripts"**—Shell scripts, collections of shell commands, are covered in this chapter.

- **Chapter 26, "SQL Data Management"**—In this chapter, you learn how to manage a SQL database.

Part VI: User Interfaces and Desktops

- **Chapter 27, "Install and Configure X11"**—Learn how to set up and modify the X11 system in this chapter.

- **Chapter 28, "Set Up a Display Manager"**—In this chapter, you learn to configure display managers such as GNOME and KDE.

- **Chapter 29, "Accessibility"**—Learn how to configure settings for individuals who have impairments.

Part VII: Administrative Tasks

- **Chapter 30, "Manage User and Group Accounts and Related System Files"**—This chapter focuses on utilities that allow you to add, modify, and delete user and group accounts.

- **Chapter 31, "Automate System Administration Tasks by Scheduling Jobs"**—Learn the process of scheduling programs and applications to run at future times.

- **Chapter 32, "Localization and Internationalization"**—In this chapter, you discover how to modify the system to behave differently in different locations throughout the world.

Part VIII: Essential System Services

- **Chapter 33, "Maintain System Time"**—In this chapter, you learn how to manage the system time, either by manually setting the time or by using a Network Time Protocol server.

- **Chapter 34, "System Logging"**—Learn how system logging is configured in this chapter.

- **Chapter 35, "Mail Transfer Agent (MTA) Basics"**—Learn how email works on Linux systems in this chapter.

- **Chapter 36, "Manage Printers and Printing"**—Learn how to set up and manage printers in this chapter.

Part IX: Networking Fundamentals

- **Chapter 37, "Fundamentals of Internet Protocols"**—In this chapter, you learn about networking essentials such as TCP/IP protocols.

- **Chapter 38, "Basic Network Configuration"**—You learn how to set up network interfaces in this chapter.

- **Chapter 39, "Basic Network Troubleshooting"**—This chapter focuses on the tools you should use to discover and fix network issues.

- **Chapter 40, "Configure Client-Side DNS"**—Learn how to configure Domain Name Service client settings in this chapter.

Part X: Security

- **Chapter 41, "Perform Security Administration Tasks"**—This chapter focuses on essential security operations.

- **Chapter 42, "Set Up Host Security"**—You learn how to securely access remote systems in this chapter.

- **Chapter 43, "Securing Data with Encryption"**—You learn how encryption tools work in Linux in this chapter.

Appendix: Create Your Own Journal

- Personalize the book to your needs by utilizing this section of blank, lined pages in the back of the book

Did I Miss Anything?

I am always interested to hear how my students—and now the readers of my books—do on both certification exams and future studies. If you would like to contact me and let me know how this book helped you in your certification goals, please do so. Did I miss anything? Let me know. Contact me at bo@OneCourseSource.com.

## CHAPTER 1

Determine and Configure Hardware Settings

This chapter provides information and commands concerning the following topics:

- /sys
- /proc
- /dev
- modprobe
- lsmod
- lspci
- lsusb

/sys

The **/sys** filesystem is designed to provide important information regarding devices and buses that the kernel is aware of. The **/sys** filesystem is memory-based, not stored on the hard drive.

Key Files and Directories in /sys

File/Directory	Description
/sys/block	Describes block devices, such as hard drives, CD-ROMs, DVDs, and RAID and LVM devices. Examples: sda (first SATA or USB drive), dm-0 (first LVM device) and sr0 (first CD-ROM or DVD).
/sys/bus	Describes devices that are attached to the system bus.
/sys/bus/cpu	Describes the CPUs that are attached to the system. Look under /sys/bus/cpu/devices to see details about each CPU.
/sys/bus/cpu /devices	Describes the USB devices that are attached to the system.

/proc

The **/proc** filesystem provides information regarding processes, kernel features, and system hardware. The **/proc** filesystem is memory-based, not stored on the hard drive.

Key Files and Directories in /proc

File/Directory	Description
/proc/cmdline	The kernel parameters that were used to boot the system.
/proc/cpuinfo	Information about the CPUs.
/proc/devices	A list of each character and block device file that the kernel has recognized.
/proc/mdstat	Information about RAID devices.
/proc/meminfo	Information about system memory.
/proc/modules	A list of all kernel modules currently loaded into memory.
/proc/partitions	The kernel's partition table. Note: this may be different from what is in the hard disk's partition table.
/proc/swaps	A list of all swap space recognized by the kernel.
/proc/vmstat	Virtual memory information.
/proc/sys	A directory that contains tunable kernel parameters.

/dev

The **/dev** filesystem contains device files. Device files are used to access physical devices (such as hard drives, keyboards, and CPUs) and virtual devices (such as LVM devices, pseudo-terminals, and software RAID devices). The **/dev** filesystem is memory-based, not stored on the hard drive.

Key Files in /dev

File	Description
/dev/sd*	Devices that begin with "sd" in the **/dev** directory are either SATA, SCSI, or USB devices. The device name **/dev/sda** refers to the first device, **/dev/sdb** refers to the second device, and so on. If a device has partitions, they are numbered starting with the value of 1.
/dev/sda1	Example: the first partition of the first SATA, SCSI, or USB device.
/dev/hd*	Devices that begin with "hd" in the **/dev** directory are IDE-based devices. The device name **/dev/hda** refers to the first device, **/dev/hdb** refers to the second device, and so on. If a device has partitions, they are numbered starting with the value of 1.
/dev/hda1	Example: the first partition of the first IDE-based device.
/dev/cdrom	Symbolic link that points to the first CD-ROM on the system.

File	Description
/dev/dm*	Devices that begin with "dm" in the /dev directory are either software RAID or LVM devices. The device name /dev/dm-0 refers to the first device, /dev/dm-1 refers to the second device, and so on.
/dev/tty*	Devices that begin with "tty" in the /dev directory are terminal devices. The device name /dev/tty0 refers to the first device, /dev/tty1 refers to the second device, and so on.

modprobe

The **modprobe** command is used to add and remove modules from the currently running kernel. Note that it also attempts to load module dependencies.

Syntax:

```
modprobe [options] [module_name]
```

Key Options for the **modprobe** Command

- **-c** displays the current **modprobe** configuration.

- **-q** runs in quiet mode.

- **-R** displays all modules that match an alias to assist you in debugging issues.

- **-r** removes the specified module from memory.

- **-v** displays verbose messages; this is useful for determining how **modprobe** is performing a task.

lsmod

The **lsmod** command displays the kernel modules that are loaded into memory.

Syntax:

```
lsmod
```

Output of the **lsmod** Command

Each line describes one module. There are three columns of information for each line:

- The module name.

- The size of the module in bytes.

- The "things" that are using the module. A "thing" could be a filesystem, a process, or another module. In the event that another module is using this module, the dependent module name is listed. Otherwise, a numeric value that indicates how many "things" use this module is provided.

Example:

```
[root@OCS ~]# lsmod | head
Module                      Size    Used by
tcp_lp                     12663    0
bnep                       19704    2
bluetooth                 372944    5 bnep
rfkill                     26536    3 bluetooth
fuse                       87741    3
xt_CHECKSUM                12549    1
ipt_MASQUERADE             12678    3
nf_nat_masquerade_ipv4     13412    1 ipt_MASQUERADE
tun                        27141    1
```

lspci

The **lspci** command displays devices that are attached to the PCI bus.

Syntax:

```
lspci [options]
```

Key Options for the lspci Command

- **-b** is "bus centric," meaning it displays IRQ (Interrupt Request Line) numbers.
- **-n** displays device numbers rather than names; names typically are stored in **/usr/share/hwdata/pci.ids** or **/usr/share/hwdata/pci.ids.gz**.
- **-nn** displays both device numbers and names.
- **-v** shows "verbose" messages.
- **-vv** shows even more "verbose" messages.
- **-vvv** shows the most "verbose" messages.

Example:

```
[root@OCS ~]# lspci
00:00.0 Host bridge: Intel Corporation 440FX - 82441FX PMC [Natoma]
(rev 02)
00:01.0 ISA bridge: Intel Corporation 82371SB PIIX3 ISA [Natoma/
Triton II]
00:01.1 IDE interface: Intel Corporation 82371AB/EB/MB PIIX4 IDE (rev 01)
00:02.0 VGA compatible controller: InnoTek Systemberatung GmbH
VirtualBox Graphics Adapter
00:03.0 Ethernet controller: Intel Corporation 82540EM Gigabit Ethernet
Controller (rev 02)
00:04.0 System peripheral: InnoTek Systemberatung GmbH VirtualBox Guest
Service
```

00:05.0 Multimedia audio controller: Intel Corporation 82801AA AC'97
Audio Controller (rev 01)

00:06.0 USB controller: Apple Inc. KeyLargo/Intrepid USB

00:07.0 Bridge: Intel Corporation 82371AB/EB/MB PIIX4 ACPI (rev 08)

00:0b.0 USB controller: Intel Corporation 82801FB/FBM/FR/FW/FRW (ICH6
Family) USB2 EHCI Controller

00:0d.0 SATA controller: Intel Corporation 82801HM/HEM (ICH8M/ICH8M-E)
SATA Controller [AHCI mode] (rev 02)

lsusb

The **lsusb** command displays devices that are attached to the PCI bus.

Syntax:

lsusb [options]

Key Options for the **lsusb** Command

- **-D** displays a specific USB device (specified as an argument) rather than probing the **/dev/bus/usb** directory and displaying all USB devices.

- **-t** displays USB devices in a tree-like format.

- **-v** shows "verbose" messages.

Example:

[root@localhost Desktop]# **lsusb**

Bus 001 Device 002: ID 1221:3234 Unknown manufacturer Disk (Thumb drive)

Bus 001 Device 001: ID 1d6b:0002 Linux Foundation 2.0 root hub

Bus 002 Device 001: ID 1d6b:0001 Linux Foundation 1.1 root hub

CHAPTER 2
Boot the System

This chapter provides information and commands concerning the following topics:

- The boot sequence from BIOS to boot completion
- Common commands for the boot loader
- Options for the kernel at boot time
- SysVinit
- Systemd
- Upstart
- Boot events in the log files
- dmesg
- BIOS
- bootloader
- kernel
- initramfs
- init

The Boot Sequence

Figure 2.1 provides an overview of the boot process.

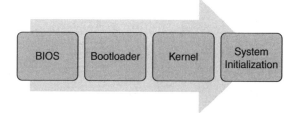

Figure 2.1 Overview of the Boot Process

Basic input/output system (BIOS) performs sanity checks, such as the power-on self test (POST), and then loads the bootloader from the master boot record (MBR).

The standard Linux bootloader is the grand unified boot loader (GRUB or GRUB2). It is responsible for loading the kernel and associated kernel modules (or *libraries*) stored in a file referred to as the **initramfs**.

The kernel is loaded from the hard disk, performs some critical boot tasks, and then passes control of the boot process to the system initialization software.

The three different system initialization systems in Linux are SysVinit (the oldest), Upstart, and Systemd (currently the most widely used). The system initialization is responsible for starting system services.

Common Commands for the Boot Loader

When booting the system, you can modify the way the boot process works by using the following commands:

Command	Description
b	Boot selected stanza.
e	Edit selected stanza or line.
c	Enter the GRUB command-line environment.
o	Open/create a new line after the current line.
O	Open/create a new line before the current line.
d	Delete the current line.
ESC	Press the Escape key to return to the main menu.

Options for the Kernel at Boot Time

The following table lists key kernel parameters to add to the "kernel" line of the boot loader. Figure 2.2 shows an example of a kernel parameter.

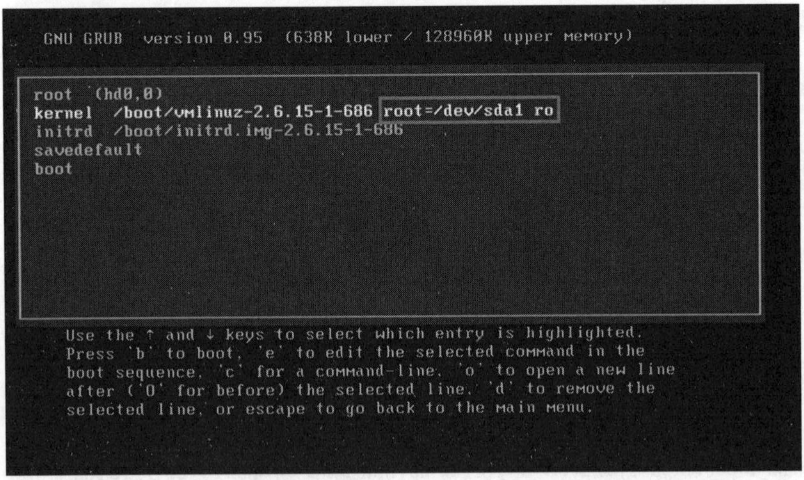

```
    GNU GRUB  version 0.95  (638K lower / 128960K upper memory)

   root  (hd0,0)
   kernel  /boot/vmlinuz-2.6.15-1-686 root=/dev/sda1 ro
   initrd  /boot/initrd.img-2.6.15-1-686
   savedefault
   boot




    Use the ↑ and ↓ keys to select which entry is highlighted.
    Press 'b' to boot, 'e' to edit the selected command in the
    boot sequence, 'c' for a command-line, 'o' to open a new line
    after ('O' for before) the selected line, 'd' to remove the
    selected line, or escape to go back to the main menu.
```

Figure 2.2   Kernel Parameters

In addition to the following parameters, dozens more are available. For a complete list of parameters, see https://www.kernel.org/doc/Documentation/kernel-parameters.txt.

Parameter	Description
quiet	Suppress normal boot messages.
single	Boot the system to single user mode.
root=	Location of the GRUB boot filesystem.
ro	Mount the GRUB boot filesystem initially as read-only (later mounted as read-write).
init=/bin/bash	Boot to a simple BASH shell.

SysVinit

The init process is started by the kernel. It reads the **/etc/inittab** file to determine which runlevel to boot the system to. This is defined by the "initdefault" line.

All sysinit lines are executed first. Then all lines that have the same value in their second field as the second field of the "initdefault" line are executed. Example: **id:5:initdefault:** means "run all lines that have the value 5 in the second field."

The **/etc/rc.d/rc.sysinit** line boots the system to "single-user" mode. The **/etc/rc.d/rc** script boots the system the rest of the way to the runlevel specified as the argument to the script. This rc (run control) script executes all files in the **/etc/rcX.d** directory (X = runlevel). Example: **/etc/rc5.d**.

All files in this directory that begin with *K* are executed with a stop argument, effectively killing or stopping the service associated with the script. Example: **/etc/rc5.d/K73ldap** stops the LDAP services if it is currently running.

All files in this directory that begin with *S* are executed with a start argument, effectively starting the service associated with the script. Example: **/etc/rc5.d/S55sshd** starts the SSH services.

All scripts in the **/etc/rcX.d** directories are actually symbolic links to scripts in the **/etc/init.d** directory. See Figure 2.3 for a visual demonstration of the SysVinit process.

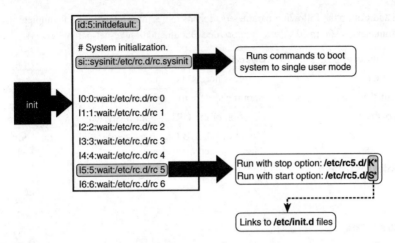

Figure 2.3   Overview of the SysVinit Process

Systemd

Instead of runlevels, Systemd uses "targets." Each target has specific services that start.
See Figure 2.4 for an example of a typical Systemd boot sequence.

Figure 2.4   Overview of the Systemd Boot Process

Targets are defined in the **/usr/lib/systemd/system** directory. Consider the following
example of a target file:

```
[root@localhost ~]# cat /usr/lib/systemd/system/graphical.target
#   This file is part of systemd.
#
#   systemd is free software; you can redistribute it and/or modify it
#   under the terms of the GNU Lesser General Public License as
published by
#   the Free Software Foundation; either version 2.1 of the License, or
#   (at your option) any later version.

[Unit]
Description=Graphical Interface
Documentation=man:systemd.special(7)
Requires=multi-user.target
Wants=display-manager.service
Conflicts=rescue.service rescue.target
After=multi-user.target rescue.service rescue.target display-manager.
service
AllowIsolate=yes
```

The default target is defined by a symbolic link from **/etc/systemd/system/ default.target** to the target in the **/usr/lib/systemd/system** directory.

Example:

```
[root@localhost ~]# ls -l /etc/systemd/system/default.target
lrwxrwxrwx. 1 root root 36 Jun 11 20:47 /etc/systemd/system/default.
target -> /lib/systemd/system/graphical.target
```

Upstart

The default boot-up runlevel is defined in the **/etc/init/rc-sysinit.conf** file. Services are defined by configuration files in the **/etc/init** directory. See Figure 2.5 for an example of an Upstart configuration file.

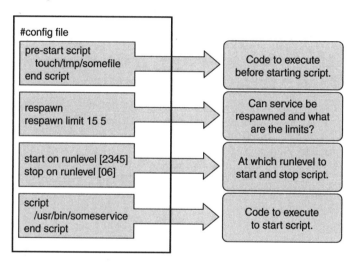

Figure 2.5   Example of an Upstart Configuration File

Boot Events in the Log Files

Here are the two locations where boot information can be found:

- **/var/log/boot.log**—System boot log
- **/var/log/dmesg**—Kernel ring buffer (or *kernel messages*)

Example of **boot.log**:

```
[root@localhost log]# more boot.log
Starting udev:                                            [  OK  ]
Setting hostname localhost.localdomain:                   [  OK  ]
Setting up Logical Volume Management:   3 logical volume(s) in volume
group "Vol Group" now active
                                                          [  OK  ]
```

```
Checking filesystems
/dev/mapper/VolGroup-lv_root: clean, 188360/1068960 files,
2692948/4287488 blocks
/dev/sda1: clean, 46/128016 files, 111454/512000 blocks
                                                        [  OK  ]
Remounting root filesystem in read-write mode:          [  OK  ]
Mounting local filesystems:                             [  OK  ]
Enabling local filesystem quotas:                       [  OK  ]
Enabling /etc/fstab swaps:                              [  OK  ]
```

dmesg

The **dmesg** command displays the in-memory copy of the kernel ring buffer.

Example:

```
[root@localhost log]# dmesg | head
Initializing cgroup subsys cpuset
Initializing cgroup subsys cpu
Linux version 2.6.32-573.7.1.el6.x86_64
(mockbuild@c6b8.bsys.dev.centos.org) (gcc version 4.4.7 20120313
(Red Hat 4.4.7-16) (GCC) ) #1 SMP Tue Sep 22 22:00:00 UTC 2015
Command line: ro root=/dev/mapper/VolGroup-lv_root rd_NO_LUKS
LANG=en_US.UTF-8 rd_NO_MD rd_LVM_LV=VolGroup/lv_swap
SYSFONT=latarcyrheb-sun16 crashkernel=auto rd_LVM_LV=VolGroup/
lv_root  KEYBOARDTYPE=pc KEYTABLE=us rd_NO_DM rhgb quiet
KERNEL supported cpus:
  Intel GenuineIntel
  AMD AuthenticAMD
  Centaur CentaurHauls
BIOS-provided physical RAM map:
  BIOS-e820: 0000000000000000 - 000000000009fc00 (usable)
```

## CHAPTER 3

Change Runlevels / Boot Targets and Shut Down or Reboot the System

This chapter provides information and commands concerning the following topics:

- Set the default runlevel or boot target
- Change between runlevels / boot targets, including single-user mode
- Shut down and reboot from the command line
- Alert users before switching runlevels / boot targets or other major system events
- Properly terminate processes
- /etc/inittab
- shutdown
- init
- /etc/init.d/
- telinit
- systemd
- systemctl
- /etc/systemd/
- /usr/lib/systemd/
- wall

Set the Default Runlevel or Boot Target

For SysVinit-based distributions, modify the second field of the initdefault line of the **/etc/inittab** file:

```
id:5:initdefault:
```

For systemd-based distributions, set the symbolic link from **default.target** to the desired target in **/lib/systemd/system:**

```
[root@localhost ~]# ln -s /etc/systemd/system/default.target /lib/
systemd/system/graphical.target
```

For Upstart-based distributions, set the **DEFAULT_RUNLEVEL** value in the **/etc/init/ rc-sysinit.conf** file:

```
env DEFAULT_RUNLEVEL=2
```

Change between Runlevels / Boot Targets, Including Single-User Mode

The following are the traditional SysVinit runlevels and Systemd targets:

Runlevel	Target	Description
0	poweroff.target	Halts the system.
1 or single	rescue.target	Single-user mode.
2	multi-user.target	Multi-user mode, traditionally with no NFS sharing or GUI.
3	multi-user.target	Multi-user mode, traditionally with no GUI.
4	Not defined	Either undefined (traditional) or a copy of runlevel 3.
5	graphical.target	Multi-user mode, traditionally with a GUI.
6	reboot.target	Reboots the system.
emergency	emergency.target	Not technically a runlevel, but a boot stage in which a very basic environment is loaded.

The following commands can be used to change the runlevels or switch to a different target:

Command	Description
init	Switches to the runlevel specified as an argument. Example: **init 1**.
telinit	Same function and syntax as the **init** command. Example: **telinit 1**.
shutdown	Brings the system down. See the "Shut Down and Reboot from the Command Line" section for additional details.
reboot	Reboots the system. See the "Shut Down and Reboot from the Command Line" section for additional details.
systemctl	Changes the current target on a Systemd-based distribution. See the "systemctl" section for additional details.

Shut Down and Reboot from the Command Line

The **shutdown** command is designed either to bring the system to a halt state or to completely power off the system. It can also be used to reboot the system. It functions on all distributions, regardless of whether it is a SysVinit, Systemd or Upstart system.

Syntax of the **shutdown** command:

```
shutdown [options] [time] [wall message]
```

Important options and arguments:

Option/Argument	Description
-H or **-halt**	Halts the system.
-P or **-poweroff**	Completely powers off the system.
-r or **-reboot**	Reboots the system.
-k	Sends a wall message but does not turn off the system. See the [wall] entry for additional details.
-c	Cancels a pending shutdown.
[**time**]	Argument to specify when to perform the shutdown operation. Time can be provided in a 24-hour clock format (for example, 20:30) or by "+m" format, where "m" is a number that represents how many minutes from now to perform the shutdown (for example, **shutdown +20**).
[**wall**]	A message to broadcast to all users who are currently logged in. This message is designed to warn users that the system will be shutting down.

Alert Users Before Switching Runlevels / Boot Targets or Other Major System Events

See the "wall" section in this chapter for details.

Properly Terminate Processes

In this context, processes refer to "services" that are controlled by SysVinit, Systemd, and Upstart. The following table details how to manage these services properly. For this table, *process* refers to the service that is being managed.

SysVinit and Upstart	Systemd	Description
service process start	**systemctl start process**	Starts the process/service.
service process stop	**systemctl stop process**	Stops the process/service.
service process restart	**systemctl restart process**	Restarts the process/service.
service process reload	**systemctl reload process**	Reloads the process/service configuration file. Useful when you're making changes to the configuration file and you don't want to restart the service.
service process status	**systemctl status process**	Displays status information about the process/service.

/etc/inittab

See the "SysVinit" section in Chapter 2, "Boot the System."

shutdown

See the "Shut Down and Reboot from the Command Line" section in this chapter for details.

init

See the "SysVinit" section in Chapter 2.

/etc/init.d/

See the "SysVinit" section in Chapter 2.

telinit

See the "Change Between Runlevels / Boot Targets, Including Single-User Mode" in this chapter for additional details.

systemd

See the "Systemd" section in Chapter 2.

systemctl

The **systemctl** command is used to change to another target on Systemd-based distributions. Example: **systemctl isolate multi-user.target**.

/etc/systemd/

See the "Systemd" section in Chapter 2.

/usr/lib/systemd/

See the "Systemd" section in Chapter 2.

wall

The **wall** command broadcasts a message to all users who are currently logged in. Syntax of the **wall** command:

```
wall [options] [<file>|<message>]
```

By default, all users can execute the **wall** command successfully because of the SGID permission placed on the executable file:

```
[root@localhost ~]# ls -l /bin/wall
-r-xr-sr-x. 1 root tty 15344 Jun  9  2014 /bin/wall
```

However, regular users cannot use the **-n** option, which is designed to remove the standard banner message:

```
[student@localhost Desktop]$ wall hello

Broadcast message from student@localhost.localdomain (pts/1) (Thu Nov 24 13:13:31 2016):

hello
[student@localhost Desktop]$ wall -n hello
wall -n: not priviliged
[student@localhost Desktop]$ su -
Password:
Last login: Thu Nov 24 09:31:04 PST 2016 on pts/0
[root@localhost ~]# wall -n hello
[root@localhost ~]#
Remote broadcast message (Thu Nov 24 13:13:48 2016):

hello
```

## CHAPTER 4

Design the Hard Disk Layout

This chapter provides information and commands concerning the following topics:

- Allocate filesystems and swap space to separate partitions or disks
- Tailor the design to the intended use of the system
- Ensure the /boot partition conforms to the hardware architecture requirements for booting
- Knowledge of basic features of LVM
- **/** (root) filesystem
- **/var** filesystem
- **/home** filesystem
- **/boot** filesystem
- Swap space
- Mount points
- Partitions

Allocate Filesystems and Swap Space to Separate Partitions or Disks

After creating a partition, you should place a filesystem on the partition. During the installation process, this step is handled automatically by the installation program. For any partitions that you create post-installation, you will have to use a tool to manually perform this task.

Several different tools can be used to create filesystems and swap space. For example, to create a filesystem, you can use the **mkfs** or **mke2fs** command. Both commands can be used to create a variety of filesystems, including XFS, btrfs, ext4, and DOS-based file-systems. To create swap space on a partition, you would use the **mkswap** command.

For details about these tools, see Chapter 17, "Create Partitions and Filesystems," which is devoted to partitions and filesystems.

Tailor the Design to the Intended Use of the System

To tailor the design of the intended use of the system, you need to consider what the system will primarily be used for. For example, your system layout (partitioning structure, software installed, and so on) will be different for a web server than a system in which developers are creating software.

To design the system, consider the following:

- What is the primary purpose of this system?

- Are there any secondary purposes for this system?

- Based on these purposes, what partition layout should be utilized? Consider the following:

    - Is there an advantage to using different filesystem types (XFS, ext4, btrfs) on different partitions?

    - Is there an advantage to using different mount options on different partitions?

    - What size should be provided to each partition?

- Should you use regular partitions, logical volume management (LVM), or software RAID devices?

- Based on the intended purpose, what software needs to be installed on the system?

Ensure the /boot Partition Conforms to the Hardware Architecture Requirements for Booting

Some bootloaders are unable to access devices that are not regular partitions. For example, traditional GRUB is not able to access LVM or software RAID devices. The **/boot** filesystem is required to be accessible by the boot loader. As a result, this filesystem should be created as a regular partition.

Knowledge of Basic features of LVM

Logical volume management (LVM) is designed to address a few issues with regular partitions, including the following:

- Regular partitions are not "resizable." LVM provides the means to change the size of partition-like structures called *logical volumes*.

- The size of a regular partition cannot exceed the overall size of the hard disk on which the partition is placed. With LVM, several physical devices can be merged together to create a much larger logical volume.

- Active filesystems pose a challenge when you're backing up data because changes to the filesystem during the backup process could result in a corrupt backup. LVM provides a feature called a "snapshot" that makes it easy to correctly back up a live filesystem.

LVM consists of one more physical devices merged into a single container of space that can be used to create partition-like devices. The physical devices can be entire hard disks, partitions on a hard disk, removable media devices (USB drives), software RAID devices, or any other storage device.

The first step in creating an LVM is to take existing physical devices and convert them into physical volumes (PVs). This is accomplished by executing the **pvcreate** command. For example, if you have three hard drives, as shown in Figure 4.1, and you want to make them all PVs, you can execute the following command:

```
pvcreate /dev/sdb /dev/sdc /dev/sdd
```

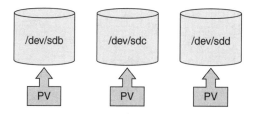

Figure 4.1   Physical Volumes

Next, place these PVs into a volume group (VG) by executing the following command:

```
vgcreate vol0 /dev/sdb /dev/sdc /dev/sdd
```

Consider a VG to be a collection of storage devices that you want to use to create partition-like structures called logical volumes. So, if **/dev/sdb** is a 60GB hard drive, **/dev/sdc** is a 30GB hard drive, and **/dev/sdd** is a 20GB hard drive, then the VG created by the previous command has 110GB of space available to create the logical volumes (LVs). You could create a single LV using all 110GB or many smaller LVs. See Figure 4.2 for a visual demonstration of volume groups.

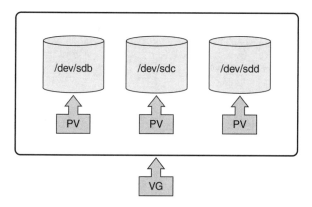

Figure 4.2   Volume Groups

The space within the PVs is broken into small chunks called *extents*. Each extent is 4MB by default (this can be modified when creating the VG by using the **-s** option to the **vgcreate** command). To create an LV, execute the **lvcreate** command and either specify how many extents to assign to the LV or provide a size (which will be rounded up to an extent size):

```
lvcreate -n lv0 -L 400MB vol0
```

The result will be a device file named **/dev/vol0/lv0** that will have 400MB of raw space available. See Figure 4.3 for a visual example.

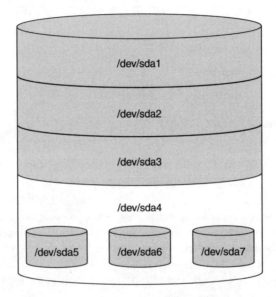

Figure 4.3   Logical Volumes

You can treat **/dev/vol0/lv0** like a regular partition, including creating a filesystem on the device and mounting it, like so:

```
mkfs -t ext4 /dev/vol0/lv0
mkdir /data
mount /dev/vol0/lv0 /data
```

/ (root) Filesystem

This is the top level of the virtual filesystem. The size of this filesystem depends greatly on which other filesystems are created.

/var Filesystem

The **/var** filesystem contains data that is variable (changes often) in nature. This includes log files, mail files, and spools (such as the print spools). The size of this filesystem depends on many factors, including whether this is a mail server, which log files are created on the system, and whether the system functions as a printer server.

/home Filesystem

The **/home** filesystem is where regular user home directories are stored. The size of this filesystem depends on many factors, including the number of users that work on the system and what functions these users perform.

/boot Filesystem

The location where the boot files—including the kernel, bootloader and initramfs files—are stored. When **/boot** is a separate filesystem, it is normally about 100–200MB in size.

Swap Space

Space on the hard disk that is used when RAM becomes full. The size of swap space is typically dependent on the size of RAM. The rule of thumb is that the swap space is normally at least equal to the size of RAM, up to double the size of RAM.

Mount Points

A mount point is a directory that is used to attach a physical filesystem to the virtual filesystem tree. Use the **mount** command to see the mount points. For example, in the following output, the **/boot** directory is a mount point for the filesystem that resides on the **/dev/sda1** partition:

```
[root@localhost ~]# mount | grep /dev/sda1
/dev/sda1 on /boot type xfs (rw,relatime,seclabel,attr2,inode64,noquota)
```

The output for the **mount** command includes the following items:

- Device name (for example, **/dev/sda1**)
- Mount point (**/boot**)
- Filesystem type (**xfs**)
- Mount options (**rw**, **realtime**, and so on)

Partitions

Partitions are used to separate a hard disk into smaller components. Each component can then be treated as a different storage device. On each partition, a separate filesystem (btrfs, xfs, etx4, and so on) can be created.

Traditional PC-based partitions have limitations regarding the number of partitions you can create. Originally only four partitions were permitted. These are referred to as *primary partitions*. As more partitions were needed, a technique was created that allowed you to convert one of the primary partitions into an extended partition. Within an extended partition, you could create additional partitions called *logical partitions*.

In Figure 4.4, **/dev/sda1**, **/dev/sda2**, and **/dev/sda3** are primary partitions. The **/dev/sda4** partition is an extended partition that is used as a container for the **/dev/sda5**, **/dev/sda6**, and **/dev/sda7** logical partitions.

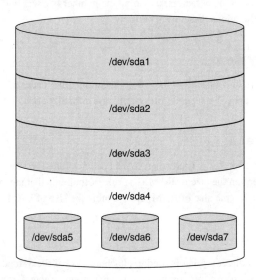

Figure 4.4 Traditional Partition Structure

On most distributions that use traditional partitions, you will be limited to a total of 15 partitions (a kernel tweak can increase this number to 63).

Traditional partition tables are stored on the master boot record (MBR). A newer partition table, called the GUID partition table (GPT), does not have the same limitations or layout that an MBR partition table has.

Several different tools can be use to create or view partitions, including **fdisk**, **parted**, and the GUI-based tool provided by the installation program. The GUI-based tool can vary based on the distribution.

Both **fdisk** and **parted** support command-line options and both can be executed as an interactive tool. For details about these tools, see Chapter 17, which is devoted to partitions and filesystems.

## CHAPTER 5

Install a Boot Manager

This chapter provides information and commands concerning the following topics:

- Providing alternative boot locations and backup boot options
- Install and configure a boot loader such as GRUB Legacy
- Perform basic configuration changes for GRUB 2
- Interact with the boot loader
- **menu.lst**, **grub.cfg**, and **grub.conf**
- **grub-install**
- **grub-mkconfig**
- MBR

Providing Alternative Boot Locations and Backup Boot Options

Typically, boot loaders are installed in the MBR. This is normally the first place the BIOS looks for the boot loader; however, if the MBR currently has a boot loader (for example, to boot Microsoft Windows on a dual-boot system), you may need to install the GRUB boot loader to the boot sector of a specific partition. This means that instead of executing the command

```
grub-install /dev/sda
```

you would execute this command instead:

```
grub-install /dev/sda1
```

Install and Configure a Boot Loader Such As GRUB Legacy

The GRUB Legacy boot loader is installed via the **grub-install** command. See the "grub-install" section of this chapter for additional details.

The configuration file for the GRUB Legacy boot loader is the **/boot/grub/grub.conf** file. See the "menu.lst, grub.cfg, and grub.conf" section of this chapter for additional details.

Perform Basic Configuration Changes for GRUB 2

GRUB 2 is configured by editing either the **/etc/default/grub** file or by editing files in the **/etc/grub.d** directory. The files in the **/etc/grub.d** directory are "advanced files" and beyond the scope of this book. These files are typically created by software developers and inserted into this directory as part of the installation of a software package.

Here's an example of a typical **/etc/default/grub** file:

```
[root@localhost ~]$ cat /boot/grub/grub.conf
GRUB_TIMEOUT=5
GRUB_DEFAULT=saved
GRUB_TERMINAL_OUTPUT="console"
GRUB_CMDLINE_LINUX="crashkernel=auto rhgb quiet"
```

Figure 5.1 describes the typical settings of the **/etc/default/grub** file.

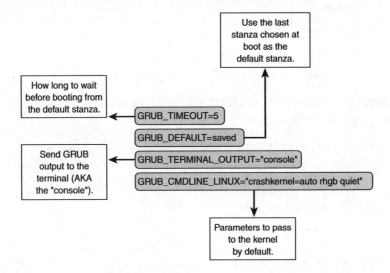

Figure 5.1   The **/etc/default/grub** Components

Interact with the Boot Loader

During the boot process, you can interact with the boot loader. This is normally useful for one of the following reasons:

- To boot to an alternative stanza
- To modify the existing boot parameters

This interaction starts with the boot menu screen, as demonstrated in Figure 5.2.

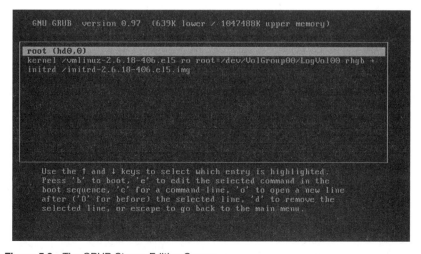

Figure 5.2   The GRUB Boot Menu Screen

The following table describes the commands available at the GRUB boot menu screen:

Command	Description
Arrow keys	Used to select a stanza.
e	Edit the currently selected stanza.
c	Enter a GRUB command prompt.
p	Only visible when a password is required to edit a stanza; use **p** to enter the required password.

If you edit a stanza, a new screen with different menu options will be provided. See Figure 5.3 for a demonstration.

Figure 5.3   The GRUB Stanza Editing Screen

The following table describes the commands available at the GRUB stanza editing screen:

Command	Description
Arrow keys	Used to select a stanza.
e	Edit the currently selected line.
c	Enter a GRUB command prompt.
o	Open (create) a new line below the current line.
O	Open (create) a new line above the current line.
d	Remove the selected line.
b	Boot the current stanza.
[ESC]	The Escape key returns you to the main menu.

menu.lst, grub.cfg, and grub.conf

The configuration file for GRUB Legacy is the **/boot/grub/grub.conf** file, shown here:

```
[root@localhost ~]$ cat /boot/grub/grub.conf
default=0
timeout=5
splashimage=(hd0,0)/grub/splash.xpm.gz
hiddenmenu
password --md5 $1$KGnIT$FU80Xxt31J1qU6FD104QF/
title CentOS (2.6.18-406.el5)
        root (hd0,0)
        kernel /vmlinuz-2.6.18-406.el5 ro root=/dev/VolGroup00/LogVol00
rhgb quiet
        initrd /initrd-2.6.18-406.el5.img
title CentOS (2.6.18-398.el5)
        root (hd0,0)
        kernel /vmlinuz-2.6.18-398.el5 ro root=/dev/VolGroup00/LogVol00
rhgb quiet
        initrd /initrd-2.6.18-398.el5.img
```

Figure 5.4 describes the key elements of this file.

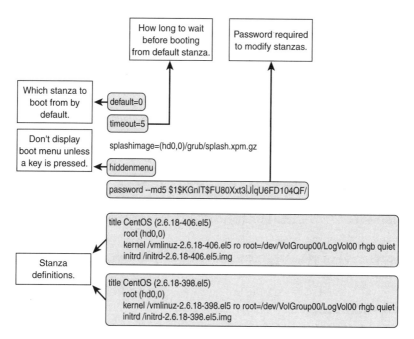

Figure 5.4   The **/boot/grub/grub.conf** File Components

A stanza in the **/boot/grub/grub.conf** file typically consists of four lines, as described in Figure 5.5.

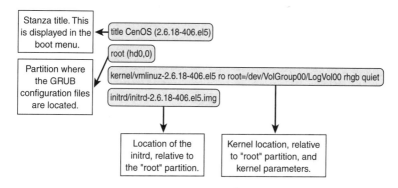

Figure 5.5   The Components of a GRUB Legacy Stanza

The GRUB2 configuration file is stored in the **/boot/grub** directory. It is either named **menu.lst** or **grub.cfg**, depending on the distribution with which you are working. These files should never be modified directly because they are generated by the **grub-mkconfig** command. See the "grub-mkconfig" section for additional details.

grub-install

The **grub-install** command installs the GRUB Legacy boot loader. In the following example, the boot loader is installed in the MBR of the first SATA hard disk:

```
grub-install /dev/sda
```

The **grub-install** command also creates configuration files in the **/boot/grub** directory.

Here are some common options:

Option	Description
--root-directory	Specify the location of the GRUB configuration files (default is **/boot**).
--force-lba	Force LBA (logical block addressing) mode

NOTE: To install the newer GRUB2 boot loader, use the following command: **grub2-install /dev/sda**.

grub-mkconfig

Only used for GRUB2, **grub-mkconfig** will generate GRUB2 configuration files from the user-editable files located in the **/etc** directory structure. This command converts data from the **/etc/default/grub** file and the files in the **/etc/grub.d** directory into the GRUB2 configuration file (either **/boot/grub/grub.cfg** or **/boot/grub/menu.lst**). See the section "Perform Basic Configuration Changes for GRUB 2" for details on the **/etc/default/grub** and **/etc/grub.d/*** files.

Figure 5.6 provides a visual example.

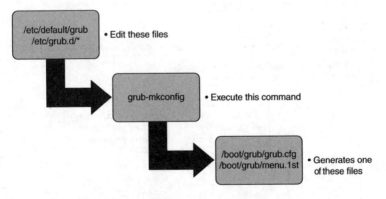

Figure 5.6   The **grub-mkconfig** Command

NOTE: On some systems, the command name is **grub2-mkconfig**.

MBR

The master boot record (MBR) is the normal location for the first-stage boot loader. By default, the BIOS looks for GRUB in the MBR to start the boot process. The MBR also holds the partition table.

You don't modify the MBR directly, but rather use a command such as **grub-install** (installs the boot loader) or **fdisk** (changes the partition table).

## CHAPTER 6

Manage Shared Libraries

This chapter provides information and commands concerning the following topics:

- Identify shared libraries
- Identify the typical locations of system libraries
- Load shared libraries
- **ldd**
- **ldconfig**
- **/etc/ld.so.conf**
- **LD_LIBRARY_PATH**

Identify Shared Libraries

Shared libraries are files used by executable programs. They are designed so developers can rely on established code to perform functions.

These shared libraries follow the naming convention lib*name*.so.*ver*, where *name* is a unique name for the library and *ver* is used to indicate the version number of the library (for example, libkpathsea.so.6.1.1).

Identify the Typical Locations of System Libraries

Normally shared library files are stored in one of the following locations on Linux distributions:

- **/lib** or **/lib64**
- **/usr/lib** or **/usr/lib64**
- **/usr/local/lib** or **/usr/local/lib64**

If your operating system is a 32-bit distribution, expect to see the libraries under **/lib**, **/usr/lib**, and **/usr/local/lib**. On 64-bit platforms, the **/lib64**, **/usr/lib/64**, and **/usr/local/lib64** directories are where you can expect to find libraries.

Load Shared Libraries

Shared libraries are loaded by C programs via the **include** statement. For example:

```
#include <stdio.h>
```

ldd

You can see what shared libraries a specific command uses by using the **ldd** command. Here is the syntax of the **ldd** command:

```
ldd [options] FILE
```

Example:

```
[root@localhost ~]# ldd /bin/cp
    linux-vdso.so.1 =>  (0x00007ffc35df9000)
    libselinux.so.1 => /lib64/libselinux.so.1 (0x00007f93faa09000)
    libacl.so.1 => /lib64/libacl.so.1 (0x00007f93fa800000)
    libattr.so.1 => /lib64/libattr.so.1 (0x00007f93fa5fa000)
    libc.so.6 => /lib64/libc.so.6 (0x00007f93fa239000)
    libpcre.so.1 => /lib64/libpcre.so.1 (0x00007f93f9fd8000)
    liblzma.so.5 => /lib64/liblzma.so.5 (0x00007f93f9db2000)
    libdl.so.2 => /lib64/libdl.so.2 (0x00007f93f9bae000)
    /lib64/ld-linux-x86-64.so.2 (0x00007f93fac42000)
    libpthread.so.0 => /lib64/libpthread.so.0 (0x00007f93f9992000)
```

The purpose of using the **ldd** command is to troubleshoot problems with code that you are writing. This command tells you not only what libraries are being called, but specifically which directory each library is being called from. This can be extremely useful when a library is not behaving as you would expect it to behave.

The following table describes useful options for the **ldd** command:

Option	Description
-v	Verbose; print additional information.
-u	Display any unused direct dependencies.

ldconfig

Used to tell the system about new locations of shared libraries, the **ldconfig** command uses information provided by the **/etc/ld.so.conf** file.

The **ldconfig** command creates a cache database of all libraries based on the configuration file. This cache is normally stored in the **/etc/ld.so.cache** file. Here is the syntax of the **ldconfig** command:

```
ldconfig [option]
```

The following table describes useful options for the **ldconfig** command:

Option	Description
-v	Verbose; print additional information.
-n	Use a command-line option to specify the location of new shared libraries. Example: **ldconfig -n /some/directory**.
-f	Specify a different configuration file rather than the default (**/etc/ld.so.conf**).
-p	Use to print a list of current libraries stored in the cache file.

Example:

```
[student@localhost Desktop]$ ldconfig -p | head
945 libs found in cache '/etc/ld.so.cache'
        p11-kit-trust.so (libc6,x86-64) => /lib64/p11-kit-trust.so
        libzapojit-0.0.so.0 (libc6,x86-64) => /lib64/libzapojit-
0.0.so.0
        libz.so.1 (libc6,x86-64) => /lib64/libz.so.1
        libyelp.so.0 (libc6,x86-64) => /lib64/libyelp.so.0
        libyaml-0.so.2 (libc6,x86-64) => /lib64/libyaml-0.so.2
        libyajl.so.2 (libc6,x86-64) => /lib64/libyajl.so.2
        libxtables.so.10 (libc6,x86-64) => /lib64/libxtables.so.10
        libxslt.so.1 (libc6,x86-64) => /lib64/libxslt.so.1
        libxshmfence.so.1 (libc6,x86-64) => /lib64/libxshmfence.so.1
```

Also see the "/etc/ld.so.conf" section in this chapter.

/etc/ld.so.conf

The primary configuration file for shared libraries is the **/etc/ld.so.conf** file; however, typically there is only a single line in this file:

```
[root@localhost ~]# more /etc/ld.so.conf
include ld.so.conf.d/*.conf
```

The **include** line in this file tells the system to also use all the configuration files in the specified directory. In the case of the previous example, that would be all the files that end in ".conf" in the **/etc/ld.so.conf.d** directory.

The configuration file itself is simple. It just contains a directory in which the shared libraries are stored:

```
[root@localhost ~]# more /etc/ld.so.conf.d/libiscsi-x86_64.conf
/usr/lib64/iscsi
[root@localhost ~]# ls /usr/lib64/iscsi
libiscsi.so.2  libiscsi.so.2.0.10900
```

To add new shared libraries to the system, you would first download the libraries to the system and place them into a directory. After adding new libraries, you would create a configuration file in the **/etc/ld.so.conf.d** directory and then execute the **ldconfig** command. All these tasks should be performed as the root user:

```
[root@localhost ~]# ls /usr/lib64/test
mylib.so.1
[root@localhost ~]# cat /etc/ld.so.conf.d/libtest.conf
/usr/lib64/test
[root@localhost ~]# ldconfig
```

If the **ldconfig** command executes successfully, there will be no output.

See Figure 6.1 for a visual demonstration of how the **ldconfig** command works.

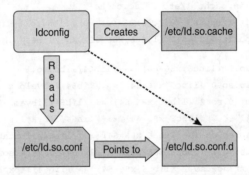

Figure 6.1 The **ldconfig** Command

LD_LIBRARY_PATH

Regular users can't successfully execute the **ldconfig** command; however, if a regular user wants to use a custom shared library, then that user can download this file into his or her home directory and make use of the **LD_LIBRARY_PATH** to indicate the location of custom library files, like so:

```
[student@localhost ~]$ ls lib
mylib.so.1
[student@localhost ~]$ LD_LIBRARY_PATH=/home/student/lib
```

If executed usefully, the last command should produce no output. To make this a permanent change, place the **LD_LIBRARY_PATH=/home/student/lib** command in your **~/.bashrc** file.

## CHAPTER 7

Use Debian Package Management

This chapter provides information and commands concerning the following topics:

- Install, upgrade, and uninstall Debian binary packages
- Find packages containing specific files or libraries that may or may not be installed
- Obtain package information such as version, content, dependencies, package integrity, and installation status (whether or not the package is installed)
- /etc/apt/sources.list
- dpkg
- dpkg-reconfigure
- apt-get
- apt-cache
- aptitude

Install, Upgrade, and Uninstall Debian Binary Packages

There are several different methods to install, upgrade, and uninstall Debian binary packages. If the package has already been downloaded, you can install or upgrade by using the **dpkg** command. See the "dpkg" section in this chapter for more information.

To download and install/upgrade a package, use the **apt-get** command or the **aptitude** menu-driven utility. See the "apt-get" and "aptitude" sections in this chapter for more information.

All three methods can be used to remove packages that are currently installed.

Find Packages Containing Specific Files or Libraries That May or May Not Be Installed

The **dpkg** command can make use of data regarding existing installed packages to determine which package "owns" a specific file or library. If the package isn't installed, the **apt-cache** command can make use of data from repositories to determine this information. See the "dpkg" and " apt-cache" sections in this chapter for more information.

Obtain Package Information Such As Version, Content, Dependencies, Package Integrity, and Installation Status (Whether or Not the Package Is Installed)

The **dpkg** command can make use of data regarding existing installed packages to determine display information regarding version, content, dependencies, and so on. If the package isn't installed, the **apt-cache** command can make use of data from repositories to determine this information. See the "dpkg" and "apt-cache" sections in this chapter for more information.

/etc/apt/sources.list

The **/etc/apt/sources.list** file contains a list of URLs of software repositories. Figure 7.1 provides a description of this file.

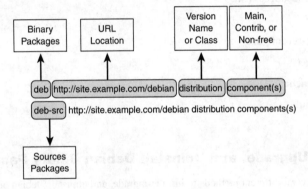

Figure 7.1   The **/etc/apt/sources.list** File

Distribution can be one of the following:

- Release name (for example, wheezy, jessie, stretch, or sid)
- Class name (for example, oldstable, stable, testing, or unstable)

Component can be one of the following:

- **main**—Packages must comply with DFSG (Debian Free Software Guidelines).
- **contrib**—Packages must comply with DFSG, but package dependencies may not.
- **non-free**—Packages do not comply with DFSG.

Example of the default file for the Jessie version of Debian:

```
deb http://httpredir.debian.org/debian jessie main
deb-src http://httpredir.debian.org/debian jessie main
```

```
deb http://httpredir.debian.org/debian jessie-updates main
deb-src http://httpredir.debian.org/debian jessie-updates main

deb http://security.debian.org/ jessie/updates main
deb-src http://security.debian.org/ jessie/updates main
```

dpkg

Use the **dpkg** command to manage local Debian packages.

Syntax of the **dpkg** command:

```
dpkg [option] command
```

Some useful options:

Option	Description
-i	Install a package.
-r	Remove the package, but keep the configuration files.
-P	Remove the package, including the configuration files (purge).
-l	List the packages currently installed.
-L	List files that were installed with a package (for example, **dpkg -L zip**).
-V	Verify the integrity of the specified package or packages.
-s	Display package status.
-C	Check for broken packages.
-S	List the package name that was responsible for a specific file being installed on the system (for example, **dpkg -S /usr/bin/zip**).

dpkg-reconfigure

When a package is installed, it may run a configuration script as part of the installation process. To run this configuration script again at some point in the future, use the **dpkg-reconfigure** command. Although there are some options to this command, they are rarely used.

Syntax of the **dpkg-reconfigure** command:

```
dpkg-reconfigure [options] source packages
```

The following example will re-run the tzdata configuration scripts:

```
dpkg-reconfigure tzdata
```

apt-get

Use the **apt-get** command to manage Debian packages that are located on a repository. This command makes use of the **/etc/apt/sources.list** file to determine which repository to use. See the "/etc/apt/sources.list" section in this chapter for more details.

Syntax examples of the **apt-get** command:

```
apt-get [options] command
apt-get [options] install|remove pkg1 [pkg2...]
apt-get [options] source pkg1 [pkg2...]
```

To specify what action to take, provide a keyword (command) to the **apt-get** command. Here are some useful commands for **apt-get**:

Command	Description
install	Installs the specified package; if the package is currently installed, use the **--only-upgrade** option to upgrade rather than install from fresh.
update	Updates the package cache of all available packages.
upgrade	Updates all packages and their dependencies.
remove	Removes a package but leaves its configuration files on the system.
purge	Removes a package, including its configuration files.

apt-cache

Use the **apt-cache** command to display package information regarding the package cache.

Syntax examples of the **apt-cache** command:

```
apt-cache [options] command
apt-cache [options] show pkg1 [pkg2...]
```

Example:

```
# apt-cache search xzip
xzip - Interpreter of Infocom-format story-files
```

To specify what action to take, provide a keyword (command) to the **apt-cache** command. Here are some useful commands for **apt-cache**:

Command	Description
Search	Displays all packages with the search term listed in the package name or description; the search term can be a regular expression.
Showpkg	Displays information about a package (package name provided as an argument).
Stats	Displays statistics about the package cache (for example, **apt-cache stats**).
Showsrc	Displays information about a source package (package name provided as an argument).
Depends	Displays a package's dependencies.
rdepends	Displays a package's reverse dependencies (packages that rely on this package).

aptitude

The **aptitude** utility is a menu-driven tool designed to make it easy to display, add, and remove packages. See Figure 7.2 for a demonstration of this tool.

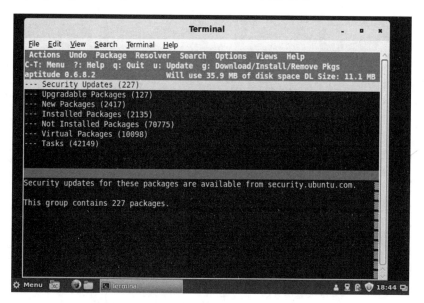

Figure 7.2   The **aptitude** Utility Screen

## CHAPTER 8

Use RPM and YUM Package Management

This chapter provides information and commands concerning the following topics:

- Install, reinstall, upgrade, and remove packages using RPM and YUM
- Obtain information on RPM packages such as version, status, dependencies, integrity, and signatures
- Determine what files a package provides, as well as find which package a specific file comes from
- **rpm**
- **rpm2cpio**
- **/etc/yum.conf**
- **/etc/yum.repos.d/**
- **yum**
- **yumdownloader**

Install, Reinstall, Upgrade, and Remove Packages Using RPM and YUM

The **rpm** command is useful for installing, upgrading, and removing packages that are already downloaded on your system. See the "rpm" section in this chapter to see additional details.

The **yum** command is useful for installing, upgrading, and removing packages that are located on a software repository. See the "yum" section in this chapter to see additional details.

Obtain Information on RPM Packages Such As Version, Status, Dependencies, Integrity, and Signatures

The **rpm** command is useful for obtaining information on RPM packages that are already downloaded on your system. See the "rpm" section in this chapter to see additional details.

The **yum** command is useful for obtaining information on RPM packages that are located on a software repository. See the "yum" section in this chapter to see additional details.

Determine What Files a Package Provides, as Well as Find Which Package a Specific File Comes From

The **rpm** command is useful for determining what files a package provides. See the "rpm" section in this chapter for additional details.

rpm

Use the **rpm** command to manage local Red Hat packages. Here are some useful options:

Option	Description
-i	Installs a package.
-U	Updates a package if an older version of the package exists; installs from scratch if the older version does not exist.
-F	Updates a package if an older version of the package exists; does nothing if an older version does not exist.
-e	Removes the package, including the configuration files.
-l	Lists packages that are currently installed.
-q	Performs a package query; additional options can be used to fine-tune the query.
-f	Determines which package a specific file belongs to.

Use the **-q** option to the **rpm** command to perform queries. Here are some additional options to fine-tune a query:

Option	Description
-a	Returns a list of all installed packages.
-c	Lists the configuration files installed with the specified package.
-d	Lists the documentation files installed with the specified package.
-i	Displays information about the specified package.
-K	Verifies the integrity of the specified package.
-l	Lists all files installed with the specified package.
-provides	Lists which capabilities the specified package provides.
-R	Lists which capabilities the specified package requires.
-s	Displays the state of each file that was installed by the specified package (normal, not installed, or replaced).

Example:

```
[student@localhost Desktop]$ rpm -qc cups
/etc/cups/classes.conf
/etc/cups/client.conf
/etc/cups/cups-files.conf
/etc/cups/cupsd.conf
/etc/cups/lpoptions
/etc/cups/printers.conf
/etc/cups/snmp.conf
/etc/cups/subscriptions.conf
/etc/dbus-1/system.d/cups.conf
/etc/logrotate.d/cups
/etc/pam.d/cups
```

rpm2cpio

The **rpm2cpio** command converts RPM files into CPIO (CPIO comes from the phrase "copy in and out") data streams. These streams can then be piped into the **cpio** command, which can extrapolate the files and directories.

Example:

```
[root@localhost package]# ls
libgcc-4.8.5-4.el7.x86_64.rpm
[root@localhost package]# rpm2cpio libgcc-4.8.5-4.el7.x86_64.rpm | cpio
-idum
353 blocks
[root@localhost package]# ls
lib64   libgcc-4.8.5-4.el7.x86_64.rpm   usr
[root@localhost package]# ls usr/share/doc/libgcc-4.8.5
COPYING   COPYING3   COPYING3.LIB   COPYING.LIB   COPYING.RUNTIME
```

This process is useful to extract specific files from an RPM file without having to reinstall the entire RPM. The resulting files are exactly the files that were installed; however, they are placed in the current directory.

There are no options or arguments for the **rpm2cpio** command. See the "cpio" section in Chapter 11, "Perform Basic File Management," for additional details regarding the **cpio** command.

/etc/yum.conf

The **/etc/yum.conf** file is the primary configuration file for **yum** commands.

Example:

```
[main]
cachedir=/var/cache/yum/$basearch/$releasever
keepcache=0
debuglevel=2
logfile=/var/log/yum.log
exactarch=1
obsoletes=1
gpgcheck=1
plugins=1
installonly_limit=5
bugtracker_url=http://bugs.centos.org/set_project.php?project_
id=23&ref=http://bugs.centos.org/bug_report_page.php?category=yum
distroverpkg=centos-release
```

Here are some key settings of the **/etc/yum.conf** file:

Setting	Description
cachedir	Directory where RPMs will be placed after download.
logfile	Location of the log file that contains **yum** actions.
gpgcheck	A value of 1 means perform a GPG (GNU Privacy Guard) check to ensure the package is valid; 0 means do not perform a GPG check. (This can be overridden by specific settings for each repository configuration file; see the "/etc/yum.repos.d" section in this chapter for more details.)
assumeyes	A value of 1 means always assume "yes" to yes/no prompts; 0 means do not make any assumption (provide a prompt instead).

/etc/yum.repos.d/

The **/etc/yum.repos.d** directory contains files that end in ".repo" and are used to specify the location of yum repositories. Each file defines one or more repositories, as described in Figure 8.1.

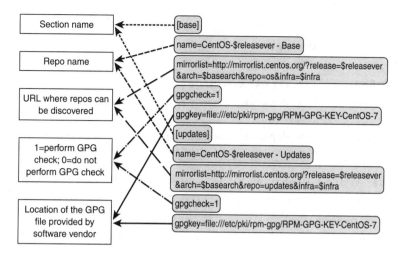

Figure 8.1   The Format of Files in the **/etc/yum.repos.d** Directory

yum

The **yum** command is used to install software from repositories. It can also be used to remove software and display information regarding software. The following table highlights the primary **yum** commands and options:

Command/Option	Description
install	Installs a package and any dependency packages from a repository. Example: **yum install zip**.
groupinstall	Installs an entire software group from a repository. Example: **yum groupinstall "Office Suite and Productivity"**.
update	Updates the specified software package.
remove	Removes the specified software package and any dependency packages from the system.
groupremove	Removes the specified software group from the system.
list	Lists information about packages, including which are installed and which are available. Example: **yum list available**.
grouplist	Lists information about software groups, including what packages are part of a group; use **yum grouplist** with no arguments to see a list of available software groups.
info	Provides information about a specific software package. Example: **yum info zip**.
groupinfo	Provides information about a specific software group.
-y	Answers "yes" automatically to any prompts. Example: **yum -y install zip**.

Important options to the **yum list** command:

Option	Description
all	Lists all packages, installed or available.
installed	Lists all packages currently installed.
available	Lists all packages currently not installed but available for installation.
updates	Lists all packages that are currently installed on the system and that also have an available newer version on a repository.

NOTE: Wild cards (or *globs*) may be used with **yum** commands. Here's an example:

```
[root@localhost ~]# yum list installed "*zip*"
Loaded plugins: fastestmirror, langpacks
Repodata is over 2 weeks old. Install yum-cron? Or run: yum makecache
fast
Loading mirror speeds from cached hostfile
 * base: mirror.supremebytes.com
 * epel: mirror.chpc.utah.edu
 * extras: mirrors.cat.pdx.edu
 * updates: centos.sonn.com
Installed Packages
bzip2.x86_64                    1.0.6-13.el7              @base
bzip2-libs.x86_64               1.0.6-13.el7              @base
gzip.x86_64                     1.5-8.el7                @base
perl-Compress-Raw-Bzip2.x86_64  2.061-3.el7              @anaconda
unzip.x86_64                    6.0-15.el7               @base
zip.x86_64                      3.0-10.el7               @anaconda
```

yumdownloader

The **yumdownloader** command is used to download software packages without installing the software. The resulting RPM file could be installed manually or copied to other systems to install.

Here are some important options to the **yumdownloader** command:

Option	Description
-destdir	Used to specify the directory to download RPM files. (The default is the current directory.)
-resolve	Used to download dependency packages for the specified package. (The default is to only download specified packages.)
-source	Used to download the source RPM, not the binary (installable) RPM.

## CHAPTER 9

Work on the Command Line

This chapter provides information and commands concerning the following topics:

- Use single shell commands and one-line command sequences to perform basic tasks on the command line
- Use and modify the shell environment, including defining, referencing, and exporting environment variables
- Use and edit the command history
- Invoke commands inside and outside the defined path
- **bash**
- **echo**
- **env**
- **export**
- **pwd**
- **set**
- **unset**
- **man**
- **uname**
- **history**
- **.bash_history**

Use Single Shell Commands and One-Line Command Sequences to Perform Basic Tasks on the Command Line

The standard way of executing a shell command is to type the command at a command prompt and then press the Enter key. For example:

```
[student@localhost rc0.d]$ pwd
/etc/rc0.d
```

To execute a sequence of commands, separate each command with a semicolon character and press the Enter key after all commands have been entered:

```
[student@localhost ~]$ pwd ; date ; ls
/home/student
Fri Dec  2 00:25:03 PST 2016
book   Desktop    Downloads  Music     Public  Templates
class  Documents  hello.pl   Pictures  rpm     Videos
```

Use and Modify the Shell Environment, Including Defining, Referencing, and Exporting Environment Variables

Shell variables are used to store information. This information is used to modify the behavior of the shell itself or external commands. The following table details some common useful shell variables:

Variable	Description
HOME	The current user's home directory.
ID	The current user's ID.
LOGNAME	The username of the user who logged in to the current session.
OLDPWD	The previous directory location (before the last **cd** command).
PATH	The location where commands are found; see the "Invoke Commands Inside and Outside the Defined Path" section for more details.
PS1	The primary prompt.
PWD	The current directory.

The **PS1** variable, for example, defines the primary prompt, often using special character sequences (**\u** = current user's name, **\h** = host name, **\W** = current directory):

```
[student@localhost ~]$ echo $PS1
[\u@\h \W]\$
```

Note that variables are defined without a dollar sign character but referenced by using the dollar sign character (**\!** = history number; see the "Use and Edit Command History" section in this chapter):

```
[student@localhost ~]$ PS1="[\u@\h \W \!]\$ "
[student@localhost ~ 93]$ echo $PS1
[\u@\h \W \!]$
```

To see all shell variables, use the **set** command, as demonstrated here:

```
[student@localhost ~ 95]$ set | head -5
ABRT_DEBUG_LOG=/dev/null
AGE=25
BASH=/bin/bash
BASHOPTS=checkwinsize:cmdhist:expand_aliases:extglob:extquote:force_
fignore:
histappend:interactive_comments:progcomp:promptvars:sourcepath
BASH_ALIASES=()
```

When a variable is initially created, it is only available in the shell where it was created. This variable is referred to as a *local variable*. In some cases, you need to pass a variable into a subprocess. This is done by using the **export** command. See the "export" section in this chapter for additional details.

Note that all variables created in the shell are temporary. To make shell variables permanent (that is, persistent across logins), see the "Customize and Use the Shell Environment" section in Chapter 23, "Find System Files and Place Files in the Correct Location."

Use and Edit Command History

Each shell keeps a list of previously executed commands in a memory-based history list. This list can be viewed by executing the **history** command (see the "history" section in this chapter for more details).

To execute a command in this list, type ! followed directly by the command you wish to execute. For example, to execute command number 84 (the **pwd** command in this example), enter the following:

```
[student@localhost ~]$ !84
pwd
/home/student
```

The following table provides some additional techniques for executing previous commands:

Technique	Description
!!	Execute the last command in the history list.
!-*n*	Execute the *n*th from the last command in the history list (for example, !-2).
!*string*	Execute the last command in the history list that begins with *string* (for example, !ls).
!?*string*	Execute the last command in the history list that has *string* anywhere in the command line (for example, !?/etc).
^*str1*^*str2*	Execute the previous command again, but replace *str1* with *str2*.

Here's an example of using ^str1^str2:

```
[student@localhost ~]$ ls /usr/shara/dict
ls: cannot access /usr/shara/dict: No such file or directory
[student@localhost ~]$ ^ra^re
ls /usr/share/dict
linux.words   words
```

Invoke Commands Inside and Outside the Defined Path

Most commands can be run by simply typing the command and pressing the Enter key. Here's an example:

```
[student@localhost ~]# date
Thu Dec  1 18:48:26 PST 2016
```

The command is "found" by using the **PATH** variable. This variable contains a comma-separated list of directory locations, as shown here:

```
[student@localhost ~]$ echo $PATH
/usr/local/bin:/usr/local/sbin:/usr/bin:/usr/sbin:/bin:/sbin:
/home/student/.local/bin:/home/student/bin
```

This "defined path" is searched in order. So, when the previous **date** command is executed, the bash shell first looks in the **/usr/local/bin** directory. If the **date** command is located in this directory, it is executed; otherwise, the next directory in the **PATH** variable is checked.

To execute a command that is not in the defined path, use a fully qualified path name, as shown here:

```
[student@localhost ~]$ /usr/xbin/xeyes
```

To add a directory to the **PATH** variable, use the following syntax:

```
[student@localhost ~]$ PATH="$PATH:/path/to/add"
```

bash

The bash shell is the standard command-line interface in Linux distributions. Several commands are built-in to the shell (rather than using a separate binary command). This chapter focuses on the most useful built-in bash shell commands.

> **NOTE:** To see details about built-in shell commands, see the man page for bash: **man bash**.

echo

The **echo** command is used to display information. Typically it is used to display the value of variables.

Example:

```
[student@localhost ~]$ echo $HISTSIZE
1000
```

The **echo** command has only a few options. The most useful one is the **-n** option, which doesn't print a newline character at the end of the output.

There are some special character sequences that can be incorporated within an argument to the **echo** command. For example, the command **echo "hello\nthere"** will send the following output:

```
hello
there
```

The following table describes some useful character sequences for the **echo** command:

Sequence	Description
\a	Ring terminal bell.
\n	Newline character.
	Tab character.
\\	A single backslash character.

env

The **env** command displays environment variables in the current shell. Local variables are not displayed when the **env** command is executed.

Another use of the **env** command is to temporarily set a variable for the execution of a command.

Example:

```
[student@localhost ~]# echo $TZ

[student@localhost ~]# date
Thu Dec  1 18:48:26 PST 2016
[student@localhost ~]# env TZ=MST7MDT date
Thu Dec  1 19:48:31 MST 2016
[student@localhost ~]# echo $TZ

[student@localhost ~]#
```

To unset a variable when executing a command, use the **--unset=VAR** option (for example, **env --unset=TZ date**).

export

To convert an existing local variable to an environment variable, use the **export** command:

```
[student@localhost ~]$ echo $NAME
Sarah
[student@localhost ~]$ export NAME
```

If the variable doesn't already exist, the **export** command can create it directly as an environment variable:

```
[student@localhost ~]$ export AGE=25
```

When a variable is converted into an environment variable, all subprocesses will have this variable set. This is useful when you want to change the behavior of a process by modifying a key variable.

For example, the **crontab -e** command allows you to edit your crontab file. To choose the editor that the **crontab** command will use, create and export the **EDITOR** variable: **export EDITOR=gedit**. See Figure 9.1 for a visual example of local versus environment variables.

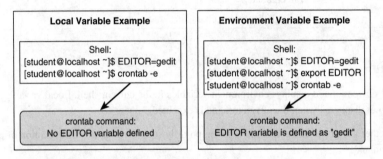

Figure 9.1   Local Versus Environment Variables

See the "crontab" section in Chapter 31, "Automate System Administration Tasks by Scheduling Jobs," for more information about **crontab**.

The **export** command can also be used to display all environment variables:

```
export -p
```

pwd

The **pwd** command is a built-in shell command that displays the shell's current directory. This command has only a couple of options, but one that is very useful is the **-P** option, which displays the "linked to" directory when you are in a directory that acts as a symbolic link.

Example:

```
[student@localhost rc0.d]$ ls -ld /etc/rc0.d
lrwxrwxrwx. 1 root root 10 Jun 11 22:15 /etc/rc0.d -> rc.d/rc0.d
[student@localhost rc0.d]$ pwd
/etc/rc0.d
[student@localhost rc0.d]$ pwd -P
/etc/rc.d/rc0.d
```

set

The set command displays all shell variables and values when executed with no arguments. The output also includes any functions that have been declared within the shell.

The set command can also be used to modify the behavior of the shell. For example, using an unset variable normally results in returning a "null string." Executing the command set -u will result in an error message when undefined variables are used:

```
[student@localhost ~]$ echo $NOPE

[student@localhost ~]$ set -u
[student@localhost ~]$ echo $NOPE
bash: NOPE: unbound variable
```

The following table provides some additional useful set options:

Option	Description
-b	When a background job terminates, report this immediately to the shell. Use +b (the default) to have this report occur before the next primary prompt is displayed.
-n	A shell programming feature that reads commands in the script but does not execute the commands. Useful for syntax error checking a script.
-u	Issue an error message when an unset variable is used.
-C	Does not allow overwriting an existing file when using redirection operators, such as cmd > file.

unset

Use the unset command to remove a variable from the shell (for example, unset VAR).

man

To discover additional information about a command, use the man page. For example, to learn more about the ls command, execute man ls.

You can use the keyboard keys to move around when viewing a man page. The following table highlights the more useful commands:

Man Page Command	Description
h	Used to display a help screen (summary of man page commands).
SPACEBAR	Move forward one page in the current document.
b	Move back one page in the current document.
ENTER	Move down one line in the current document; the down-arrow key can also perform this operation.
UP ARROW	Move up one line in the current document.
/term	Search the document for term (this can be a regular expression or just plain text).
q	Quit the man page and return to the shell.

Because of the large number of man pages, they are broken into categories called "sections." In some cases, the section will need to be included as an argument. For example, **man passwd** (the man page for the **passwd** command) will produce a different document than **man 5 passwd** (the man page for the **/etc/passwd** file). The primary sections are detailed in the following table:

Section	Description
1	Executable commands and shell commands
2	System calls
3	Library calls
4	Special files (a.k.a. device files in /dev)
5	File formats
6	Games
7	Miscellaneous
8	System administrator-based commands
9	Kernel routines

This next table provides some useful man page options:

Option	Description
-k	Used to search the man page database for documents that match a keyword, which can be a regular expression or plain text (for example, **man -l password**).
-f	Displays a brief summary of a command.
-w	Displays the location of the man page.
-M	Used to specify an alternative location for man pages.

To specify an alternative man page location, you can use the **-M** option or create a **MANPATH** variable.

Syntax:

```
[student@localhost ~]$ MANPATH=/opt/man
```

uname

The **uname** command displays system information. Here are some useful options:

Option	Description
-a	Displays all information
-s	Displays the kernel name
-n	Displays the network node (a.k.a. the host name)
-r	Displays the release version of the kernel
-v	Displays the version (date) of the kernel
-m	Displays the machine hardware name (often the same as **-p**)
-p	Displays the processor type (often the same as **-m**)
-o	Displays the operating system

Example:

```
[student@localhost ~]$ uname -a
Linux localhost.localdomain 3.10.0-327.18.2.el7.x86_64 #1 SMP Thu May
12 11:03:5
```

history

The **history** command displays the contents of the history command list. This output can be quite large, so often a numeric value is given to limit the number of commands displayed. For example, the following **history** command lists the last five commands in the history list:

```
[student@localhost ~]$ history 5
   83  ls
   84  pwd
   85  cat /etc/passwd
   86  clear
   87  history 5
```

Here are some useful options:

Option	Description
-c	Clear the history list for the current bash shell.
-r	Read the contents of the history file (see the ".bash_history" section in this chapter) and use those contents to replace the history list of the current bash shell.
-w	Write the history list of the current bash shell to the history file (see the ".bash_history" section in this chapter).

Several variables can affect how information is stored in the history list:

Variable	Description
HISTIGNORE	A list of patterns, separated by colons, that indicates what commands to *not* place in the history list. For example, the following would have no **cd**, **pwd**, and **clear** commands placed in the history list: **HISTIGNORE="cd*:pwd;clear"**
HISTSIZE	Set to a numeric value that represents the maximum number of commands to keep in the history list.
HISTCONTROL	Limits the lines that are stored in the history list. This can be set to one of the following: **ignorespace**—Any command executed with a space in front of it is not placed in the history list. **ignoredups**—Duplicated commands result in only one occurrence place in the history list. **ignoreboth**—Combines **ignorespace** and **ignoredups**. **erasedups**—The next write to the history list also removes all duplicate entries in the current history list.

.bash_history

When a user logs off the system, the current history list is written automatically to the user's **.bash_history** file. This is typically stored in the user's home directory (**~/.bash_history**), but the name and location can be changed by modifying the **HISTFILE** variable.

How many lines are stored in the **.bash_history** file is determined by the value of the **HISTFILESIZE** variable.

## CHAPTER 10

Process Text Streams Using Filters

This chapter provides information and commands concerning the following topics:

- cat
- cut
- expand
- fmt
- head
- join
- less
- nl
- od
- paste
- pr
- sed
- sort
- split
- tail
- tr
- unexpand
- uniq
- wc

cat

The **cat** command displays the contents of text files. Important options include the following:

Option	Description
-A	Same as **-vET**.
-e	Same as **-vE**.
-E	Displays a $ character at the end of each line (used to see trailing whitespace characters).

Option	Description
-n	Numbers all lines of output.
-s	Converts multiple blank lines into a single blank line.
-T	Displays "^I" characters for each tab character (used to see spaces instead of tabs).
-v	Displays "unprintable" characters (such as control characters).

cut

The **cut** command is used to display "sections" of data. Important options include the following:

Option	Description
-b	Used to define a section to print by bytes.
-c	Used to define a section to print by characters.
-d	Used to specify a delimiter character (used with the -f option).
-f	Used to specify which fields to display.

Example using fields:

```
[student@localhost ~]$ head -2 /etc/passwd
root:x:0:0:root:/root:/bin/bash
bin:x:1:1:bin:/bin:/sbin/nologin
[student@localhost ~]$ head -2 /etc/passwd | cut -d: -f1,7
root:/bin/bash
bin:/sbin/nologin
```

Example using characters:

```
[student@localhost ~]$ ls -l /etc/passwd
-rw-r--r--. 1 root root 2607 Nov  3 10:15 /etc/passwd
[student@localhost ~]$ ls -l /etc/passwd | cut -c1-10,42-
-rw-r--r-- /etc/passwd
```

expand

The **expand** command converts tabs into spaces. Use the **-t** option to specify how many spaces to insert in place of each tab.

Example:

```
[student@localhost ~]$ cat -T sample.txt
Example:^IOne
Test:^I^ITwo
[student@localhost ~]$ expand -t 4 sample.txt
Example:    One
Test:       Two
[student@localhost ~]$ expand -t 8 sample.txt
Example:        One
Test:           Two
```

NOTE: The -T option to the **cat** command is used to display tabs using ^I to represent a tab.

fmt

The **fmt** command performs simple formatting of text data. Important options include the following:

Option	Description
-u	Changes the document so there is only one space between each word and two spaces after each sentence.
-w	Used to specify the maximum number of characters in each line.

Example:

```
[student@localhost ~]$ cat data.txt
pam_motd — Display the motd file


DESCRIPTION


pam_motd is a PAM module that can be used to display arbitrary motd
(message of the day) files after a successful login. By default
the /etc/motd file is shown. The message size is limited to 64KB.


[student@localhost ~]$ fmt -w 40 data.txt
pam_motd — Display the motd file


DESCRIPTION


pam_motd is a PAM module that can be
used to display arbitrary motd (message
of the day) files after a successful
login. By default the /etc/motd file
is shown. The message size is limited
to 64KB.
```

head

The **head** command displays the top part of text data. By default, the top ten lines are displayed. Use the **-n** option to display a different number of lines:

```
[student@localhost ~]$ ls -l | head -3
total 12
drwxrwxr-x. 2 student student   6 Aug 22 16:51 book
drwxrwxr-x. 2 student student   6 Aug 22 16:51 class
```

join

The **join** command merges files into a single file by using a common field. The two files must already be sorted on the common field before the **join** command is run. See Figure 10.1 for an example.

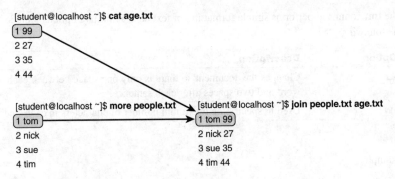

Figure 10.1   Using the **join** Command

less

The **less** command is used to display large chunks of text data. Unlike the **cat** command, the **less** command will pause after displaying the first page of information. Keys on the keyboard allow the user to scroll through the document. The following table highlights the more useful movement keys:

Movement Key	Description
h	Displays a help screen (summary of the **less** command movement keys).
SPACEBAR	Move forward one page in the current document.
b	Move back one page in the current document.
ENTER	Move down one line in the current document; the down-arrow key can also perform this operation.
UP ARROW	Move up one line in the current document.

Movement Key	Description
/term	Search the document for *term* (this can be a regular expression or just plain text).
q	Quit viewing the document and return to the shell.

nl

The **nl** command displays a file with numbered lines.

od

The **od** command "dumps" files into either octal format or another format. By default, it converts data into octal format:

```
[student@localhost ~]$ more people.txt
1 tom
2 nick
3 sue
4 tim
[student@localhost ~]$ od people.txt
0000000 020061 067564 005155 020062 064556 065543 031412 071440
0000020 062565 032012 072040 066551 000012
0000031
```

Important options include the following:

Option	Description
-t	Used to specify the output format: "d" for decimal, "f" for floating point, and "x" for hexadecimal.
-N *x*	Limits the output to *x* number of bytes.

paste

The **paste** command is used to merge files together. See Figure 10.2 for an example.

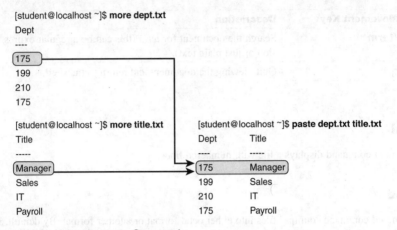

Figure 10.2   Using the **paste** Command

Use the **-d** option to specify the output delimiter (the default is a tab character).

pr

The **pr** command is used to perform changes to text before it's sent to a printer. Important options include the following:

Option	Description
-l	Used to indicate how many lines appear per page of output (for example, **pr -l 44 file.txt**).
-t	Suppresses the page header; the header includes a timestamp and the page number.
-d	Double-space the output.
-o	Used to specify the indent value (for example, **pr -o 8 file.txt**).
-w	Used to specify the maximum width (number of characters) of each line.

sed

Use the **sed** utility to make automated modifications to files. The basic format for the **sed** command is **sed** *'s/RE/string/' file*.

The "RE" refers to the term *regular expression*, a feature that uses special characters to match patterns. See Chapter 15, "Search Text Files Using Regular Expressions," for more details about regular expressions.

Example of the **sed** command:

```
[student@localhost ~]$ head -n 5 /etc/passwd
root:x:0:0:root:/root:/bin/bash
bin:x:1:1:bin:/bin:/sbin/nologin
daemon:x:2:2:daemon:/sbin:/sbin/nologin
adm:x:3:4:adm:/var/adm:/sbin/nologin
lp:x:4:7:lp:/var/spool/lpd:/sbin/nologin
[student@localhost ~]$ head -n 5 /etc/passwd | sed 's/bin/----/'
root:x:0:0:root:/root:/----/bash
----:x:1:1:bin:/bin:/sbin/nologin
daemon:x:2:2:daemon:/s----:/sbin/nologin
adm:x:3:4:adm:/var/adm:/s----/nologin
lp:x:4:7:lp:/var/spool/lpd:/s----/nologin
```

sed is a very powerful utility with a large number of features. The following table describes some of the more useful **sed** utilities:

Feature	Description
'/RE/d'	Deletes lines that match the RE from the output of the **sed** command.
'/RE/c*string***'**	Changes lines that match the RE to the value of *string*.
'/RE/a*string***'**	Add *string* on a line after all lines that match the RE.
'/RE/i*string***'**	Add *string* on a line before all lines that match the RE.

The **sed** command has two important modifiers (characters added to the end of the **sed** operation):

- **g**—Means "global." By default only the first RE pattern match is replaced. When the **g** modifier is used, all replacements are made. See Figure 10.3 for an example.

```
[student@localhost ~]$ head -n 5 /etc/passwd | sed 's/bin/----/'
root:x:0:0:root:/root:/----/bash
----:x:1:1:bin:/bin:/sbin/nologin
daemon:x:2:2:daemon:/s----:/sbin/nologin
adm:x:3:4:adm:/var/adm:/s----/nologin
lp:x:4:7:lp:/var/spool/lpd:/s----/nologin
[student@localhost ~]$ head -n 5 /etc/passwd | sed 's/bin/----/g'
root:x:0:0:root:/root:/----/bash
----:x:1:1:----:/----:/s----/nologin
daemon:x:2:2:daemon:/s----:/s----/nologin
adm:x:3:4:adm:/var/adm:/s----/nologin
lp:x:4:7:lp:/var/spool/lpd:/s----/nologin
```

Figure 10.3 The **g** Modifier

- **i**—Means "case-insensitive." This modifier matches an alpha character regardless of its case. So, the command **sed 's/a/-/i'** would match either "a" or "A" and replace it with the "-" character.

The **sed** command can also change the original file (instead of displaying the modified data to the screen). To change the original file, use the **-i** option.

sort

The **sort** command can be use to sort text data. By default, it will break each line of data into fields, using whitespace as the default delimiter. It also sorts on the first field in the data by default, performing a dictionary sort:

```
[student@localhost ~]$ cat individuals.txt
tom
nick
sue
Tim
[student@localhost ~]$ sort individuals.txt
nick
sue
Tim
tom
```

Important options include the following:

Option	Description
-f	Fold case (essentially case-insensitive).
-h	Human-based numeric sort (for example, 2K is lower than 1G).
-n	Numeric sort.
-M	Month-based sort.
-r	Used to reverse the sort order.
-t	Used to change the field separator (for example, **sort -t ":" file.txt**).
-u	Used to remove duplicate lines.

To sort on a different field than the default, use the **-k** option. Here's an example:

```
[student@localhost ~]$ more people.txt
1 tom
2 nick
3 sue
4 tim
```

```
[student@localhost ~]$ sort -k 2 people.txt
2 nick
3 sue
4 tim
1 tom
```

split

To break up a large file into a series of smaller files, use the **split** command. In the following example, the **linux.words** file is split into smaller files of 100,000 lines each. Each file is named **x--**, where "--" is **aa**, **ab**, **ac**, and so on.

```
[student@localhost dictionary]$ ls
linux.words
[student@localhost dictionary]$ split -l 100000 linux.words
[student@localhost dictionary]$ ls
linux.words   xaa   xab   xac   xad   xae
```

Important options include the following:

Option	Description
-b	Break up files based on the number of bytes in each file (for example, **split -b 5000 file.txt**).
-l	Break a file into smaller files based on the number of lines per file; the default is set to 1,000.

To use a different prefix than "x", add a second argument:

```
[student@localhost dictionary]$ ls
linux.words
[student@localhost dictionary]$ split -l 100000 linux.words words
[student@localhost dictionary]$ ls
linux.words   wordsaa   wordsab   wordsac   wordsad   wordsae
```

tail

The **tail** command displays the bottom part of text data. By default, the last ten lines are displayed. Use the **-n** option to display a different number of lines:

```
[student@localhost ~]$ cal 1999 | tail -n 9
       October                November                December
Su Mo Tu We Th Fr Sa    Su Mo Tu We Th Fr Sa    Su Mo Tu We Th Fr Sa
                1  2        1  2  3  4  5  6              1  2  3  4
 3  4  5  6  7  8  9     7  8  9 10 11 12 13     5  6  7  8  9 10 11
10 11 12 13 14 15 16    14 15 16 17 18 19 20    12 13 14 15 16 17 18
17 18 19 20 21 22 23    21 22 23 24 25 26 27    19 20 21 22 23 24 25
24 25 26 27 28 29 30    28 29 30                26 27 28 29 30 31
```

Important options include the following:

Option	Description
-f	Display the bottom part of a file and follow changes means to continue to display any changes made to the file.
-n +x	Display from line number x to the end of the file.

tr

The **tr** command is useful for translating characters from one set to another. The syntax of the command is **tr** *SET1* [*SET2*].

For example, the following will capitalize the output of the **date** command:

```
[student@localhost dictionary]$ date
Sat Dec  3 20:15:05 PST 2016
[student@localhost dictionary]$ date | tr 'a-z' 'A-Z'
SAT DEC  3 20:15:18 PST 2016
```

Note that in order to use the **tr** command on a file, you must redirect the file into the **tr** command, like so, because the **tr** command does not accept files as arguments:

```
tr 'a-z' 'A-Z' < file
```

Important options include the following:

Option	Description
-d	Used when the second set is omitted; it deletes the matching characters. For example, the following deletes all numbers from the output of the **date** command: **date	tr -d '0-9'**.
-s	Repeated matching characters are converted into a single character before being translated. Thus, "aaabc" would be converted into "abc" and then translated to "Abc" if the command **tr -s 'a' 'A'** were executed.

unexpand

The **unexpand** command converts spaces into tabs. Use the **-t** option to specify how many consecutive spaces to convert into tabs.

uniq

The **uniq** command will remove duplicated lines from a sorted file:

```
[student@localhost ~]$ cat names.txt
adm
bin
bin
operator
root
root
root
shutdown
[student@localhost ~]$ uniq names.txt
adm
bin
operator
root
shutdown
```

For the **uniq** command to work correctly, the file must first be sorted. Because the **sort** command has a "unique only" option (see the "sort" section in this chapter for details), it is more common to use the **sort** command, rather than the **uniq** command, to remove duplicates.

However, the **uniq** command has an interesting feature in that it will report how many duplicate lines were present; this feature is not available with the **sort** command:

```
[student@localhost ~]$ uniq -c names.txt
      1 adm
      2 bin
      1 operator
      3 root
      1 shutdown
```

wc

Used to display the number of lines, words, or characters of data. By default, all three values are displayed:

```
[student@localhost ~]$ wc sample.txt
2   4 24 sample.txt
```

Important options include the following:

Option	Description
-c	Only display the number of bytes. (For text data, a byte is one character.)
-m	Only display the number of characters.
-l	Only display the number of lines.
-w	Only display the number of words.

## CHAPTER 11

Perform Basic File Management

This chapter provides information and commands concerning the following topics:

- Copy, move, and remove files and directories individually
- Copy multiple files and directories recursively
- Remove files and directories recursively
- Use simple and advanced wildcard specifications in commands
- Using **find** to locate and act on files based on type, size, or time
- Usage of tar, cpio, and dd
- **cp**
- **find**
- **mkdir**
- **mv**
- **ls**
- **rm**
- **rmdir**
- **touch**
- **tar**
- **cpio**
- **dd**
- **file**
- **gzip**
- **gunzip**
- **bzip2**
- **xz**
- File globbing

Copy, Move, and Remove Files and Directories Individually

See the "cp," "mv," and "rm" sections in this chapter for details.

Copy Multiple Files and Directories Recursively

To copy multiple files, use a file glob in conjunction with the **cp** command. See the "File Globbing" section in this chapter for further details.

To copy directories recursively, use the **-r** option to the **cp** command. See the "cp" section in this chapter for further details.

Remove Files and Directories Recursively

To copy multiple files, use a file glob in conjunction with the **rm** command. See the "File Globbing" section in this chapter for further details.

To copy directories recursively, use the **-r** option to the **rm** command. See the "rm" section in this chapter for further details.

Use Simple and Advanced Wildcard Specifications in Commands

See the "File Globbing" section in this chapter for details.

Using find to Locate and Act on Files Based on Type, Size, or Time

See the "find" section in this chapter for details.

Usage of tar, cpio, and dd

See the "tar," "cpio," and "dd" sections in this chapter for details.

cp

The **cp** command is used to copy files or directories. Here's the syntax for this command:

```
cp [options] file|directory destination
```

The *file|directory* is which file or directory to copy. The *destination* is where to copy the file or directory to. The following example copies the **/etc/hosts** file into the current directory:

```
[student@localhost ~]$ cp /etc/hosts .
```

Note that the destination *must* be specified.

The following table provides some important options for the **cp** command:

Option	Description
-i	Provide an interactive prompt if the copy process results in overwriting an existing file.
-n	Never overwrite an existing file.
-r	Copy the entire directory structure ("r" stands for recursive)
-v	Be verbose (describe actions taken when copying files and directories).

find

The **find** command will search the live filesystem for files and directories using different criteria. Here's the format of the command:

```
find [options] starting_point criteria action
```

The *starting_point* is the directory to start the search from. The *criteria* is what to search for, and the *action* is what to do with the results.

The following options are designed to modify how the **find** command behaves:

Option	Description
-maxdepth *n*	Limits how deep into subdirectories the search goes; for example, **find-maxdepth 3** will limit the search to three subdirectories deep.
-mount	Prevents searching directories that serve as mount points. This is useful when you're searching from the / directory.
-regextype *type*	When regular expressions (RE) are used, this option specifies what type of RE will be used; *type* can be emacs (default), posix-awk, posix-basic, posix-egrep, or posix-extended.

Most criteria-based options allow you to specify a numeric value as an argument. This can be preceded by a - or + character to indicate "less than" or "greater than." For example, using **+5** would mean "more than five." Here are some important criteria-based options:

Option	Description
-amin *n*	Matches files based on access time; for example, **-amin -3** would match files accessed within the past three minutes.
-group *name*	Matches files that are owned by the *name* group.
-name *pattern*	Matches a file or directory based on the *pattern* provided; the *pattern* can be a regular expression.
-mmin *n*	Matches files based on modification time; for example, **-mmin -3** would match files modified within the past three minutes.
-nogroup	Matches files not owned by a group.

Option	Description
-nouser	Matches files not owned by a user.
-perm *mode*	Matches files that match the permission specified by the *mode* (octal or symbolic); see the examples in the next table.
-size *n*	Matches files based on file size; the value *n* can be preceded by a + (more than) or − (less than) and anteceded by a unit modifier: **c** for bytes, **k** for kilobytes, **M** for megabytes, or **G** for gigabytes.
-type *fstype*	
-user *username*	Matches all files owned by the *username* user (for example, **find /home -user bob**).

Examples using the **-perm** option:

Option	Description
-perm 775	Matches files that exactly match the octal permissions of 775 (rwxrwxr-x).
-perm u=rw	Matches files that exactly match the symbolic permissions of read and write for the owner (rw-------).
-perm -444	Matches files that match the octal permissions of 444 but disregards any other permission values (possible matches: rwxrwxr-x, r--r--r--, rwxr--r--).
-perm ugo=r	Matches files that match the symbolic permissions of read for all three permission sets but disregards any other permission values (possible matches: rwxrwxr-x, r--r--r--, rwxr--r--).
-perm /444	Matches files that match any of the octal permissions of 444 and disregards any other permission values (possible matches: r--------, rw-rw-r--, rwxr--r--).

Once a file is found, an action can be taken on the file. Here are some important action-based options:

Option	Description
-delete	Delete all matched files (for example, **find /tmp -name "*.tmp" -delete**).
-exec *command*	Execute a command on each matched file (see the following example).
-ls	List details about each matched file.
-ok	Execute a command on each matched file, but prompt the user before each match; prompt is a yes/no question to determine if the user wants to execute the command.
-print	Print the filename of each matched file; this is the default action option.

Here's an example of the **-exec** option:

```
[root@localhost ~]# find /etc -name "*.cfg" -exec file {} \;
/etc/grub2.cfg: symbolic link to '../boot/grub2/grub.cfg'
/etc/enscript.cfg: ASCII text
/etc/python/cert-verification.cfg: ASCII text
```

The **\;** is used to build a command line. For example, the command that was executed for the previous **find** example was **file /etc/grub2.cfg; file /etc/enscript.cfg; file /etc/python/cert-verification.cfg**. The \ before the **;** is required to escape the meaning of the **;** character for the bash shell, so the **;** character is passed to the **find** command as a regular argument.

The **{}** characters represent where in the command the matching filename is placed. This can be used more than once, as demonstrated in the next example, which makes a copy of each matched file:

```
find /etc -name "*.cfg" -exec cp {} /tmp/{}.bak \;
```

mkdir

The **mkdir** command creates a directory.

Example:

```
mkdir test
```

Important **mkdir** options:

Option	Description
-m *perm*	Sets the permissions for the new directory rather than using the umask value.
-p	Creates parent directories if necessary; for example, **mkdir /home/bob/data/january** would create all the directories in the path if they don't exist.
-v	Is verbose by printing a message for every directory that is created.

mv

The **mv** command will move or rename a file.

Example:

```
mv /tmp/myfile ~
```

Important options include the following:

Option	Description
-i	Provide an interactive prompt if the move process would result in overwriting an existing file.
-n	Never overwrite an existing file.
-v	Be verbose (describe actions taken when moving files and directories).

ls

The **ls** command is used to list files in a directory. Important options include the following:

Option	Description
-a	List all files, including hidden files.
-d	List directory name, not the contents of the directory.
-F	Append a character to the end of the file to indicate its type; examples include *=executable file, /=directory, and @=symbolic link file.
-h	When used with the -l option, file sizes are provided in human-readable sizes.
-i	Display each file's inode value.
-l	Display long listing (see the example after this table).
-r	Reverse the output order of the file listing.
-S	Sort by file size.
-t	Sort by modification time (newest files are listed first).

The output of the **ls -l** command includes one line per file, as demonstrated in Figure 11.1.

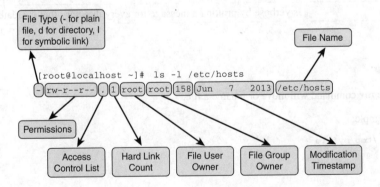

Figure 11.1   The *ls -l* Command

rm

The **rm** command is used to delete files and directories.

Example:

```
rm file.txt
```

Important options include the following:

Option	Description
-i	Provides an interactive prompt before removing file.
-r	Deletes entire directory structure. ("r" stands for recursive.)
-v	Is verbose (describes actions taken when deleting files and directories).

rmdir

The **rmdir** command is used to delete empty directories. This command will fail if the directory is not empty (use **rm -r** to delete a directory and all the files within the directory).

Example:

```
rmdir data
```

touch

The **touch** command has two functions: to create an empty file and to update the modification and access timestamps of an existing file. To create a file or update an existing file's timestamps to the current time, use the following syntax:

```
touch filename
```

Important options include the following:

Option	Description
-a	Modify the access timestamp only, not the modification timestamp.
-d DATE	Set the timestamp to the specified DATE (for example, **touch -d "2018-01-01 14:00:00"**).
-m	Modify the modification timestamp only, not the access timestamp.
-r file	Use the timestamp of file as a reference to set the timestamps of the specified file (for example, **touch -r /etc/hosts /etc/passwd**).

tar

The purpose of the **tar** command is to merge multiple files into a single file. To create a tar file named **sample.tar**, execute the following:

```
tar -cf sample.tar files_to_merge
```

To list the contents of a .tar file:

```
tar -tf sample.tar
```

To extract the contents of a .tar file:

```
tar -xf sample.tar
```

Important options include the following:

Option	Description
-c	Create a .tar file.
-t	List the contents of a .tar file.
-x	Extract the contents of a .tar file.
-f	Specify the name of the .tar file.
-v	Be verbose (provide more details as to what the command is doing).
-A	Append new files to an existing .tar file.
-d	Compare the difference between a .tar file and the files in a directory.
-u	Update; only append newer files into an existing .tar file.
-j	Compress/uncompress the .tar file using the **bzip2** utility.
-J	Compress/uncompress the .tar file using the **xz** utility.
-z	Compress/uncompress the .tar file using the **gzip** utility.

cpio

The purpose of the **cpio** command is to create archives. You can create an archive of files by sending the filenames into the command as STDIN, as in the following example:

```
[student@localhost ~]$ find /etc -name "*.conf" | cpio -ov > conf.cpio
```

Important options include the following:

Option	Description
-d	Used with the **-i** option to extract the directory structure as well as the files in the **cpio** file.
-i	Extract data from a **cpio** file; the file should be provided via STDIN (for example, **cpio -i < conf.cpio**).
-o	Create an archive (output file).
-t	List table of contents of a **cpio** file.
-v	Verbose mode.

dd

The **dd** command can perform multiple operations related to backing up data and creating files. One common use is to make a backup of an entire drive; for example, the following backs up the entire **/dev/sdb** device to the **/dev/sdc** device:

```
[student@localhost ~]$ dd if=/dev/sdb of=/dev/sdc bs=4096
```

Another use of the **dd** command is to create a large file that can be used as a swap file:

```
[student@localhost ~]$ dd if=/dev/zero of=/var/swapfile bs=1M count=50
```

Important options include the following:

Option	Description
if=	Specify the input file.
of=	Specify the output file.
bs=	Specify the block size.
count=	Indicate the number of blocks to create/transfer.

file

The **file** command will report the type of contents in the file. Here are some examples:

```
[student@localhost ~]$ file /etc/hosts
/etc/hosts: ASCII text
[student@localhost ~]$ file /usr/bin/ls
/usr/bin/ls: ELF 64-bit LSB executable, x86-64, version 1 (SYSV),
dynamically linked (uses shared libs), for GNU/Linux 2.6.32,
BuildID[sha1]=aa7ff68f13de25936a098016243ce57c3c982e06, stripped
[student@localhost ~]$ file /usr/share/doc/pam-1.1.8/html/sag-author.html
/usr/share/doc/pam-1.1.8/html/sag-author.html: HTML document,
UTF-8 Unicode text, with very long lines
```

gzip

Use the **gzip** command to compress files:

```
[student@localhost ~]$ ls -lh juju
-rwxr-xr-x 1 vagrant vagrant 109M Jan 10 09:20 juju
[student@localhost ~]$ gzip juju
[student@localhost ~]$ ls -lh juju.gz
-rwxr-xr-x 1 vagrant vagrant 17M Jan 10 09:20 juju.gz
```

Note that the **gzip** command replaces the original file with the compressed file.

Important options include the following:

Option	Description
-c	Write output to STDOUT and do not replace original file. Use redirection to place output data into a new file (for example, **gzip -c juju > juju.gz**).
-d	Decompress the file (you can also use the **gunzip** command).
-r	Recursive: Used when a directory argument is given to compress all files in the directory (and its subdirectories).
-v	Verbose: Display percentage of compression.

The **gzip**, **xz**, and **bzip2** commands are very similar. The biggest difference is the technique used to compress files. The **gzip** command uses the Lempel-Ziv coding method, whereas the **bzip2** command uses the Burrows-Wheeler block-sorting text-compression algorithm and Huffman coding. The **xz** command uses the LZMA and LZMA2 compression methods.

gunzip

Use the **gzip** command to decompress gzipped files:

```
[student@localhost ~]$ ls -lh juju.gz
-rwxr-xr-x 1 vagrant vagrant 17M Jan 10 09:20 juju.gz
[student@localhost ~]$ gunzip juju
[student@localhost ~]$ ls -lh juju
-rwxr-xr-x 1 vagrant vagrant 109M Jan 10 09:20 juju
```

bzip2

Use the **bzip2** command to compress files:

```
[student@localhost ~]$ ls -lh juju
-rwxr-xr-x 1 vagrant vagrant 109M Jan 10 09:20 juju
[student@localhost ~]$ bzip2 juju
[student@localhost ~]$ ls -lh juju.bz2
-rwxr-xr-x 1 vagrant vagrant 14M Jan 10 09:20 juju.bz2
```

Note that the **bzip2** command replaces the original file with the compressed file.

Important options include the following:

Option	Description
-c	Write output to STDOUT and do not replace original file. Use redirection to place output data into a new file (for example, **bzip2 -c juju > juju.bz**).
-d	Decompress the file (you can also use the **bunzip2** command).
-v	Verbose: Display percentage of compression.

The **gzip**, **xz**, and **bzip2** commands are very similar. The biggest difference is the technique used to compress files. The **gzip** command uses the Lempel-Ziv coding method, whereas the **bzip2** command uses the Burrows-Wheeler block-sorting text-compression algorithm and Huffman coding. The **xz** command uses the LZMA and LZMA2 compression methods.

xz

Use the **xz** command to compress files:

```
[student@localhost ~]$ ls -lh juju
```

```
-rwxr-xr-x 1 vagrant vagrant 109M Jan 10 09:20 juju
[student@localhost ~]$ xz juju
[student@localhost ~]$ ls -lh juju.xz
-rwxr-xr-x 1 vagrant vagrant 11M Jan 10 09:20 juju.xz
```

Important options include the following:

Option	Description
-c	Write output to STDOUT and do not replace original file. Use redirection to place output data into a new file (for example, **xz -c juju > juju.xz**).
-d	Decompress the file (you can also use the **unxz** command).
-l	List information about an existing compressed file (for example, **xz -l juju.xz**).
-v	Verbose: Display percentage of compression.

The **gzip**, **xz**, and **bzip2** commands are very similar. The biggest difference is the technique used to compress files. The **gzip** command uses the Lempel-Ziv coding method, whereas the **bzip2** command uses the Burrows-Wheeler block-sorting text-compression algorithm and Huffman coding. The **xz** command uses the LZMA and LZMA2 compression methods.

File Globbing

A file glob (also called a *wildcard*) is any character provided on the command line that represents a portion of a filename. The following globs are supported:

Glob	Description
*	Matches zero or more characters in a filename.
?	Matches any single character in a filename.
[ ]	Matches a single character in a filename as long as that character is represented within the [ ] characters.

This example copies all files that end in **.txt**:

```
[student@localhost ~]$ cp *.txt ~
```

The next example will remove all files that are four characters long:

```
[student@localhost ~]$ rm ????
```

To view the file type for all files in the current directory that begin with **a**, **b**, or **c**, execute the following command:

```
[student@localhost ~]$ file [abc]*
```

The previous command could also be executed in the following manner:

```
[student@localhost ~]$ file [a-c]*
```

The **a-c** represents a range of characters. This must be a valid range within the ASCII text table. To view this table, execute the following command:

```
[student@localhost ~]$ man ascii
```

Multiple ranges or lists of values are permitted:

```
[student@localhost ~]$ file [a-cg-jz]*
```

By placing a **!** character at the beginning of the range, you specify what characters cannot match. For example, the following command will copy all files in the current directory that don't begin with an **a**, **b**, or **c**:

```
[student@localhost ~]$ cp [!abc]* ~
```

The previous example also demonstrates that complex patterns can be created using multiple glob characters.

## CHAPTER 12

Use Streams, Pipes, and Redirects

This chapter provides information and commands concerning the following topics:

- Redirecting standard input, standard output, and standard error
- Pipe the output of one command to the input of another command
- Use the output of one command as arguments to another command
- Send output to both STDOUT and a file
- **tee**
- **xargs**

Redirecting Standard Input, Standard Output, and Standard Error

Each command is able to send two streams of output (standard output and standard error) and can accept one stream of data (standard input). In documentation, these terms can also be described using the following:

- Standard output = STDOUT or STDOUT
- Standard error = stderr or STDERR
- Standard input = STDIN or STDIN

By default, STDOUT and stderr are sent to the terminal window, whereas STDIN comes from keyboard input. In some cases you want to change these locations, and this is accomplished by a process called *redirection*.

The following table describes the methods used to perform redirection:

Method	Description
cmd < file	Override STDIN so the input comes from the file specified.
cmd > file	Override STDOUT so the output goes into the file specified.
cmd 2> file	Override stderr so the output goes into the file specified.
cmd &> file	Override both STDOUT and stderr so the output goes into the file specified.
cmd1 | cmd2	Override STDOUT from *cmd1* so it goes into *cmd2* as STDIN. See the "Pipe the Output of One Command to the Input of Another Command" section for more details regarding this feature.

In the following example, STDOUT of the **cal** program is sent to a file named **month**:

```
[student@localhost ~]$ cal > month
```

It is common to redirect both STDOUT and stderr into separate files, as demonstrated in the next example:

```
[student@localhost ~]$ find /etc -name "*.cfg" -exec file {} \;
> output 2> error
```

Redirecting STDIN is fairly rare because most commands will accept a filename as a regular argument; however, the **tr** command, which performs character translations, requires redirecting STDIN:

```
[student@localhost ~]$ cat /etc/hostname
localhost
[student@localhost ~]$ tr 'a-z' 'A-Z' < /etc/hostname
LOCALHOST
```

Pipe the Output of One Command to the Input of Another Command

The process of piping (called piping because the | character is referred to as a "pipe") the output of one command to another command results in a more powerful command line. For example, the following takes the standard output of the **ls** command and sends it into the **grep** command to filter files that were changed on April 16th:

```
[student@localhost ~]$ ls -l /etc | grep "Apr 16"
-rw-r--r-- 1 root root     321 Apr 16  2014 blkid.conf
drwxr-xr-x 2 root root    4096 Apr 16  2014 fstab.d
```

In the next example, lines 41–50 of the copyright file are displayed:

```
[student@localhost ~]$ head -50 copyright | tail
        b) If you have received a modified Vim that was distributed as
           mentioned under a) you are allowed to further distribute it
           unmodified, as mentioned at I). If you make additional changes
           the text under a) applies to those changes.
        c) Provide all the changes, including source code, with every
           copy of the modified Vim you distribute. This may be done in
           the form of a context diff. You can choose what license to use
           for new code you add. The changes and their license must not
           restrict others from making their own changes to the official
           version of Vim.
        d) When you have a modified Vim which includes changes as
           mentioned
```

You can add additional commands as demonstrated here:

```
[student@localhost ~]$ head -50 copyright | tail | nl
     1    b) If you have received a modified Vim that was distributed as
     2       mentioned under a) you are allowed to further distribute it
     3       unmodified, as mentioned at I). If you make additional changes
     4       the text under a) applies to those changes.
     5    c) Provide all the changes, including source code, with every
     6       copy of the modified Vim you distribute. This may be done in
     7       the form of a context diff. You can choose what license
to use
     8       for new code you add. The changes and their license must not
     9       restrict others from making their own changes to the official
    10       version of Vim.
    11    d) When you have a modified Vim which includes changes as
    12       mentioned
```

Note that the order of execution makes a difference. In the previous example, the first 40 lines of the copyright file are sent to the **tail** command. Then the last ten lines of the first 40 lines are sent to the **nl** command for numbering. Notice the difference in output when the **nl** command is executed first:

```
[student@localhost ~]$ nl copyright | head -50 | tail
    36    b) If you have received a modified Vim that was distributed as
    37       mentioned under a) you are allowed to further distribute it
    38       unmodified, as mentioned at I). If you make additional changes
    39       the text under a) applies to those changes.
    40    c) Provide all the changes, including source code, with every
    41       copy of the modified Vim you distribute. This may be done in
    42       the form of a context diff. You can choose what license to use
    43       for new code you add. The changes and their license must not
    44       restrict others from making their own changes to the official
    45       version of Vim.
    45    d) When you have a modified Vim which includes changes as
    47       mentioned
```

Use the Output of One Command as Arguments to Another Command

To take the output of one command and use it as an argument to another command, place the command within the **$( )** characters. For example, the output of the **date** and **pwd** commands is sent to the **echo** command as arguments:

```
[student@localhost ~]$ echo "Today is $(date) and you are in the
$(pwd) directory"
Today is Tue Jan 10 12:42:02 UTC 2017 and you are in the /home/student
directory
```

Send Output to Both STDOUT and a File

See the "tee" section in this chapter for details.

tee

If you want STDOUT to be sent both to the terminal and to a file, send the output to the **tee** command and provide an argument to the **tee** command that indicates the file you want to store the information in. Here's an example:

```
[student@localhost ~]$ ls
[student@localhost ~]$ cal | tee cal.txt
     January 2017
Su Mo Tu We Th Fr Sa
 1  2  3  4  5  6  7
 8  9 10 11 12 13 14
15 16 17 18 19 20 21
22 23 24 25 26 27 28
29 30 31

[student@localhost ~]$ ls
cal.txt
```

The **tee** command only has a few options. The most useful is the **-a** option. By default, the **tee** command will completely overwrite the file; the **-a** option tells the **tee** command to append to the file.

xargs

The **xargs** command takes data from STDIN to build and execute commands. Here is the format of the command:

input_command | **xarg** *execute_command*

The *input_command* is designed to provide information for **xargs** to provide as arguments to the *execute_command*. For example, suppose you want to run the **wc -l** command on every file in the **/etc** directory that begins with the letter "e":

```
[student@localhost ~]$ ls -d /etc/e* | xargs wc -l
1 /etc/ec2_version
1 /etc/environment
2 total
```

Important options for the **xargs** command include the following:

Option	Description
-0	Handles whitespace issues. Normally used to handle when filenames have whitespace characters; every character is treated as a literal character.
-d	Used to change the delimiter between arguments (default is a space character).
-n *max-args*	Indicates the maximum number of arguments per *execute_command*.
-p	Prompts the user before executing the *execute_command*.
-t	Displays the *execute_command* command before executing the command.

## CHAPTER 13

Create, Monitor, and Kill Processes

This chapter provides information and commands concerning the following topics:

- Run jobs in the foreground and background
- Signal a program to continue running after logout
- Monitor active processes
- Select and sort processes for display
- Send signals to processes
- **&**
- **bg**
- **fg**
- **jobs**
- **kill**
- **nohup**
- **ps**
- **top**
- **free**
- **uptime**
- **pgrep**
- **pkill**
- **killall**

Run Jobs in the Foreground and Background

Typically processes are started as foreground jobs. When a process is in the foreground, the bash shell from which the process was launched is not available. A process that is run in the background leaves the bash shell available for the user to execute additional commands.

The terms *job* and *process* are essentially interchangeable. Any program running on the system is a process. A job is a process that is executed from the command line. Each bash shell keeps track of jobs that were launched from that shell.

For additional information on running foreground and background jobs, see the "&," "bg," and "fg" sections in this chapter.

Signal a Program to Continue Running After Logout

See the "nohup" section in this chapter for details.

Monitor Active Processes

See the "ps," "top," and "pgrep" sections in this chapter for details.

Select and Sort Processes for Display

See the "ps," "top," and "pgrep" sections in this chapter for details.

Send Signals to Processes

See the "kill," "top," "pkill," and "killall" sections in this chapter for details.

&

By default, processes started on the command line are run in the foreground. This means that the bash shell is not accessible until the process that is running in the foreground is terminated.

Running a process in the background allows you to continue to work in the bash shell and execute additional commands. To execute a process in the background, add an **&** character to the end of the command, like so:

```
[student@localhost ~]$ xeyes &
```

bg

A paused process can be restarted in the background by using the **bg** command:

```
[student@localhost ~]$ jobs
[1]+  Stopped                 sleep 999
[student@localhost ~]$ bg %1
[1]+ sleep 999 &
[student@localhost ~]$ jobs
[1]+  Running                 sleep 999 &
```

> **NOTE:** You can pause a process that is running in the foreground by holding down the Ctrl button and pressing Z while in that process's window.

For more information about the **jobs** command, see the "jobs" section in this chapter.

fg

A paused process can be restarted in the foreground by using the **fg** command:

```
[student@localhost ~]$ jobs
[1]+  Stopped                    sleep 999
[student@localhost ~]$ fg %1
sleep 999
```

NOTE: You can pause a process that is running in the foreground by holding down the Ctrl button and pressing Z while in that process's window.

For more information about the jobs command, see the "jobs" section in this chapter.

jobs

Each bash shell keeps track of the processes that are running from that shell. These processes are referred to as *jobs*. To list the currently running jobs, execute the **jobs** command from the bash shell, like so:

```
[student@localhost ~]$ jobs
[1]-  Running                    sleep 999 &
[2]+  Running                    sleep 777 &
```

Each job is assigned a job number that controls the job. Refer to this job number using the following syntax: *%job_number*.

kill

The **kill** command can be used to change the state of a process, including stopping (killing) it. To stop a process, first determine its process ID or job number and then provide that number as an argument to the **kill** command:

```
[student@localhost ~]$ jobs
[1]-  Running                    sleep 999 &
[2]+  Running                    sleep 777 &
[student@localhost ~]$ kill %2
[student@localhost ~]$ jobs
[1]-  Running                    sleep 999 &
[2]+  Terminated                 sleep 777
[student@localhost ~]$ ps -fe | grep sleep
student   17846 12540  0 14:30 pts/2    00:00:00 sleep 999
student   17853 12540  0 14:31 pts/2    00:00:00 grep --color=auto sleep
[student@localhost ~]$ kill 17846
[student@localhost ~]$ ps -fe | grep sleep
student   17856 12540  0 14:31 pts/2    00:00:00 grep --color=auto sleep
[1]+  Terminated                 sleep 999
```

Important options include the following:

Option	Description
-9	Force kill. Used when the process doesn't exit when a regular kill command is executed.
-l	Used to provide a list of other numeric values that can be used to send different kill signals to a process.

nohup

Each process has a parent process that started it. For example, if you execute a command in a bash shell, then that command's parent process is the bash shell process.

When a parent process is stopped, a hang up (HUP) signal is sent to all the child processes. This HUP signal is designed to stop the child processes. By default, a child process will stop when sent a HUP signal.

To avoid this, execute the child process with the **nohup** command:

```
[student@localhost ~]$ nohup some_command
```

This technique is typically used when you remotely log in to a system and want to have some command continue to run even if you are disconnected. When you are disconnected, all of the programs you have running are sent HUP signals. Using the **nohup** command allows this specific process to continue running.

ps

The **ps** command is used to list processes that are running on the system. With no arguments, the command will list any child process of the current shell as well as the bash shell itself, as shown here:

```
[student@localhost ~]$ ps
  PID TTY          TIME CMD
18360 pts/0    00:00:00 bash
18691 pts/0    00:00:00 ps
```

The **ps** command is unusual in that it supports older BSD options that normally don't have a "-" character in front of them.

Important options include the following:

Option	Description
-e	Display all processes running on the system; the BSD method of **ps ax** can also be used.
-f	Display full information (additional information about each process).
-u *username*	Display all processes owned by *username*.
-forest	Provide a process hierarchy tree.

top

The **top** command displays process information that is updated on a regular basis (by default, every 2 seconds). The first half of the output of the **top** command contains overall information, whereas the second half displays a select list of processes (by default, the processes that are using the CPU the most).

Figure 13.1 shows some typical output of the **top** command.

```
top - 16:09:10 up 2 days,  3:07,  2 users,  load average: 0.00, 0.07, 0.12
Tasks: 119 total,   2 running, 117 sleeping,   0 stopped,   0 zombie
%Cpu(s):  1.3 us,  1.0 sy,  0.0 ni, 97.0 id,  0.3 wa,  0.0 hi,  0.3 si,  0.0 st
KiB Mem:   4048292 total,  3832140 used,   216152 free,   356468 buffers
KiB Swap:        0 total,        0 used,        0 free.  1610568 cached Mem

  PID USER      PR  NI    VIRT    RES    SHR S %CPU %MEM     TIME+ COMMAND
26159 root      20   0 2461400 1.243g  24040 S  2.7 32.2  44:59.94 java
  965 root       0 -20       0      0      0 S  0.3  0.0   0:35.58 loop0
27545 nobody    20   0   87524   3616    892 S  0.3  0.1   0:05.32 nginx
28770 root      20   0   12824    940    776 S  0.3  0.0   0:14.39 ping
    1 root      20   0   33604   2952   1476 S  0.0  0.1   0:00.98 init
    2 root      20   0       0      0      0 S  0.0  0.0   0:00.00 kthreadd
    3 root      20   0       0      0      0 S  0.0  0.0   0:05.72 ksoftirqd/0
    5 root       0 -20       0      0      0 S  0.0  0.0   0:00.00 kworker/0:0H
    7 root      20   0       0      0      0 S  0.0  0.0   1:12.43 rcu_sched
    8 root      20   0       0      0      0 R  0.0  0.0   1:39.49 rcuos/0
    9 root      20   0       0      0      0 S  0.0  0.0   0:00.00 rcu_bh
   10 root      20   0       0      0      0 S  0.0  0.0   0:00.00 rcuob/0
   11 root      rt   0       0      0      0 S  0.0  0.0   0:00.00 migration/0
```

Figure 13.1   The *top* Command Output

The following table describes the output displayed in Figure 13.1.

Output	Description
First line	Output derived from the **uptime** command; see the "uptime" section for further details.
Second line	A summary of processes running on the system.
Third line	CPU statics since the last time top data was refreshed.
Fourth line	Physical memory statics. (Note: Type **E** while in the **top** command to change the value from kilobytes to another value.)
Fifth line	Virtual memory statics.
Remaining lines	A list of processes and associated information.

While the **top** command is running, you can use interactive commands to perform actions such as change display values, reorder the process list, and kill processes. These interactive commands are single characters. The more important interactive commands are provided in the following table:

Command	Description
h	Help. Display a summary of interactive commands.
E	Change the default value from kilobytes to another value; values "cycle" around back to kilobytes.
Z	Toggle color highlighting on; use lowercase z to toggle color and non-color.
B	Toggle bold on and off.
< >	Move the sort column to the left (<) or the right (>).
s	Set the update value to a different value than the default of 2 seconds.
k	Kill a process by providing a process ID (PID).
q	Quit the **top** command.

The **top** command also supports several command-line options. Important options include the following:

Option	Description
-d	Set the time between data refresh.
-n *number*	Maximum number of data refreshes until the **top** command exits.
-u *username*	Display only processes owned by *username*.

free

The **free** command displays memory statistics:

```
[student@localhost ~]$ free
              total       used       free     shared    buffers     cached
Mem:        4048292    3891592     156700        460     370640    1617812
-/+ buffers/cache:      1903140    2145152
Swap:             0          0          0
```

Important options include the following:

Option	Description
-k	Display memory usage in kilobytes.
-m	Display memory usage in megabytes.
-g	Display memory usage in gigabytes.
-s *n*	Update the display every *n* seconds.
-t	Display a line that shows the total of each column.

uptime

The **uptime** command displays how long the system has been up for and its load average:

```
[student@localhost ~]$ uptime
 15:06:13 up 2 days,  9:09,  3 users,  load average: 0.01, 0.02, 0.05
```

The load average indicates the CPU usage over the last 1, 5, and 15 minutes (0.01, 0.02 and 0.05, for example). Load average is related to the number of CPUs, as described here:

- A load average of 1.0 on a single CPU system means 100% utilization.

- A load average of 2.0 on a single CPU system means 200% utilization (meaning that processes were often waiting for the CPU because it was busy).

- A load average of 1.0 on a system with two CPUs means 50% utilization.

- A load average of 2.0 on a system with two CPUs means 100% utilization.

pgrep

Typically you utilize a combination of the **ps** and **grep** commands to display specific processes:

```
[student@localhost ~]$ ps -e | grep sleep
25194 pts/0    00:00:00 sleep
```

However, the **pgrep** command can provide similar functionality:

```
[student@localhost ~]$ pgrep sleep
25194
```

Important options for **pgrep** include the following:

Option	Description
-G *name*	Match processes by group name.
-l	Display process name and PID.
-n	Display most recently started processes first.
-u *name*	Match processes by user *name*.

pkill

When sending signals to a process using the **kill** command, you indicate which process by providing a process ID (PID). With the **pkill** command, you can provide a process name, a user name, or other methods to indicate which process or processes to send a signal. For example, the following will send a kill signal to all processes owned by the user sarah:

```
[student@localhost ~]$  pkill -u sarah
```

Important options for **pkill** include the following:

Option	Description
-G *name*	Match processes by group *name*
-u *name*	Match processes by user *name*

killall

The **killall** command is used to stop all the processes of a specific name:

```
[student@localhost ~]$  killall firefox
```

Important options for **killall** include the following:

Option	Description
-I	Case-insensitive match.
-i	Interactive. Prompt before sending the signal to the process.
-r *pattern*	Match processes by regular expression *pattern*.
-s *signal*	Send *signal* to process instead of the default signal.
-v	Verbose. Report if the process was successfully sent the signal.

Modify Process Execution Priorities

This chapter provides information and commands concerning the following topics:

- Know the default priority of a job that is created
- Run a program with a higher or lower priority than the default
- Change the priority of a running process
- **nice**
- **ps**
- **renice**
- **top**

Know the Default Priority of a Job That Is Created

Nice values are used to indicate to the CPU which process has the higher priority for access to the CPU. The values range from –20 (highest priority) to 19 (lowest priority). The default priority of any job created by a user is 0. See the "nice" section in this chapter for details on how to set a different priority when executing a command.

Run a Program with Higher or Lower Priority than the Default

See the "nice" section in this chapter for details.

Change the Priority of a Running Process

See the "renice" section in this chapter for details.

nice

To specify a different nice value than the default, execute the job via the **nice** command:

```
[student@localhost ~]$ nice -n 5 firefox
```

Note that regular users cannot assign a negative nice value. These values can only be used by the root user. There are no additional useful options besides the **-n** option.

To view the nice value of a process, use the **-o** option with the **ps** command and include the value of "nice":

```
[student@localhost ~] ps -o nice,pid,cmd
NI    PID CMD
 0  23865 -bash
 0  27969 ps -o nice,pid,cmd
```

ps

See the "ps" section in Chapter 13, "Create, Monitor, and Kill Processes," for details.

renice

Use the **renice** command to change the nice value of an existing job:

```
[student@localhost ~] ps -o nice,pid,cmd
NI    PID CMD
 0  23865 -bash
 5  28235 sleep 999
 0  28261 ps -o nice,pid,cmd
[student@localhost ~] renice -n 10 -p 28235
28235 (process ID) old priority 5, new priority 10
[student@localhost ~] ps -o nice,pid,cmd
NI    PID CMD
 0  23865 -bash
10  28235 sleep 999
 0  28261 ps -o nice,pid,cmd
```

NOTE: Regular (non-root) users can only change the priority of an existing process to a lower priority. Only the root user can alter a process priority to a higher priority.

Important options include the following:

Option	Description
-g *group*	Change the priority of all files owned by *group*.
-u *user*	Change the priority of all files owned by *user*.

top

See the "top" section in Chapter 13, "Create, Monitor, and Kill Processes," for details.

## CHAPTER 15

Search Text Files Using Regular Expressions

This chapter provides information and commands concerning the following topics:

- Create simple regular expressions containing several notational elements
- Use regular expression tools to perform searches through a filesystem or file content
- **grep**
- **egrep**
- **fgrep**
- **sed**
- **regex(7)**

Create Simple Regular Expressions Containing Several Notational Elements

See the "regex(7)" section in this chapter for additional details regarding creating regular expressions.

Use Regular Expression Tools to Perform Searches through a Filesystem or File Content

To search the filesystem based on parameters such as the name of the file, use the **find** command. The **find** command supports the **-regexp** option, which allows you to use regular expressions to perform pattern matching of the filename.

Example:

```
[student@localhost ~]$ find / -regex ".*chpasswd.*8.*" 2> /dev/null
/usr/share/man/zh_CN/man8/chpasswd.8.gz
/usr/share/man/ja/man8/chpasswd.8.gz
/usr/share/man/zh_TW/man8/chpasswd.8.gz
/usr/share/man/ru/man8/chpasswd.8.gz
/usr/share/man/de/man8/chpasswd.8.gz
/usr/share/man/fr/man8/chpasswd.8.gz
/usr/share/man/man8/chpasswd.8.gz
/usr/share/man/it/man8/chpasswd.8.gz
```

See the "find" section in Chapter 11, "Perform Basic File Management," for more details about the **find** command. See the "regex(7)" section in this chapter for additional details regarding regular expressions.

To search the filesystem based on file content, use the **grep** command using the **-r** option.

Example:

```
[student@localhost ~]$ grep -r ":[0-9][0-9]:games:" /etc 2> /dev/null
/etc/passwd:games:x:5:60:games:/usr/games:/usr/sbin/nologin
```

See the "grep" section in this chapter for more details about the **grep** command. See the "regex(7)" section in this chapter for additional details regarding regular expressions.

grep

Use the **grep** command to search files for lines that contain a specific pattern. By default, the **grep** command will display the entire line when it finds a matching pattern.

Example:

```
[student@localhost ~]$ grep "the" /etc/rsyslog.conf
# To enable high precision timestamps, comment out the following line.
# Set the default permissions for all log files.
```

NOTE: The pattern used to perform the search uses basic regular expressions. See the "regex(7)" section in this chapter for additional details regarding basic regular expressions.

Important options for the **grep** command include the following:

Option	Description
-c	Display a count of the number of matching lines rather than displaying each line that matches.
-color	The text that matches is displayed in a different color than the rest of the text.
-E	Use extended regular expressions in addition to basic regular expressions. See the "regex(7)" section in this chapter for additional details regarding extended regular expressions.
-f	Fixed strings; all characters in the pattern will be treated as regular characters, not regular expression characters.
-e	Used to specify multiple patterns in one **grep** command (for example, **grep -e** *pattern1* **-e** *pattern2 file*).
-f *file*	Use patterns found within the specified *file*.
-i	Ignore case.
-l	Display filenames that match the pattern, rather than displaying every line in the file that matches. This is useful when you're searching multiple files (for example, **grep "the" /etc/***).

Option	Description
-n	Display the line number before displaying the line.
-r	Recursively search all the files in a directory structure.
-v	Inverse match; return all lines that don't contain the pattern specified.
-w	Match whole words only; for example, the command **grep "the"** *file* will match the letters "the" even when part of a larger word such as "then" or "there", but the command **grep -w "the"** *file* will only match "the" as a separate word.

egrep

The **egrep** command performs the same function as the **grep -E** command. See the "grep" section in this chapter for additional details.

fgrep

The **fgrep** command performs the same function as the **grep -f** command. See the "grep" section in this chapter for additional details.

sed

The **sed** command is designed to edit file data in a non-interactive method. Unlike most editors (such as the vi editor), which require human interaction to perform modification to files, the **sed** command can make changes automatically.

In the following example, the **sed** command will replace "localhost" with "myhost" in the **/etc/hosts** file:

```
[student@localhost ~]$ cat /etc/hosts
127.0.0.1 localhost
[student@localhost ~]$ sed 's/localhost/myhost/' /etc/hosts
127.0.0.1 myhost
```

Only the first occurrence on each line is replaced by default. To have all occurrences replaced, use the **/g** modifier, as shown in the next example:

```
[student@localhost ~]$ sed 's/0/X/' /etc/hosts
127.X.0.1 localhost
[student@localhost ~]$ sed 's/0/X/g' /etc/hosts
127.X.X.1 localhost
```

Note that the search pattern can be a regular expression (basic only, by default). See the "regex(7)" section in this chapter for additional details regarding regular expressions.

The **sed** command does not replace the original file. Redirect output into another file, like so:

```
[student@localhost ~]$ sed 's/0/X/' /etc/hosts > myhosts
```

Important operations for the **sed** command include the following:

Operation	Description
s/	Substitute.
d	Delete; for example, the following would delete any line that contained "enemy": **sed '/enemy/d'** *filename*.
a\	Append data after the matching line (for example, **sed '/localhost/ a**).
i\	Insert data before the matching line.

Important options for the **sed** command include the following:

Option	Description
-f *file*	Use **sed** commands that are located in *file*.
-i	Edit the file in place; be careful, this will replace the original file with the modifications.
-r	Use extended regular expressions in addition to basic regular expressions. See the "regex(7)" section in this chapter for additional details regarding extended regular expressions.

regex(7)

The term *regex* stands for regular expression (RE), which is a character or set of characters designed to match other characters. For example, in utilities that support REs, a "." character will match a single character of any type, whereas "[a-z]" would match any single lowercase character.

There are two types of REs: basic and extended. Basic REs are the original and extended REs are the newer additions. Utilities that use REs normally support basic REs by default and have some switch or feature to enable extended REs. Although documentation may refer to basic REs as obsolete, they are still used by most modern utilities.

Commonly used basic REs are described in the following table:

RE	Description
^	Match the beginning of a line.
$	Match the end of a line.
*	Match the preceding character zero or more times.
.	Match exactly one character.
[ ]	Match exactly one character that is within the [ ] characters; a list of characters ([abc]) or a range of characters ([a-c]) is permitted.
[^]	Match exactly one character that is *not* within the [ ] characters; a list of characters ([^abc]) or a range of characters ([^a-c]) is permitted.
\	Escape the special meaning of a regular expression; for example, the pattern \.* would match the value ".*".

Commonly used extended REs are described in the following table:

RE	Description
( )	Group sets of characters together to form an expression; for example, (abc).
X|*Y*	Match either *X* or *Y*.
+	Match the preceding character or expression one or more times.
{X}	Match the preceding character or expression *X* times.
{X,}	Match the preceding character or expression *X* or more times.
{X,Y}	Match the preceding character or expression *X* to *Y* times.
?	The previous character or expression is optional.

Note that the (7) in the title of this section refers to the man page that contains information about REs: **man 7 regex**.

## CHAPTER 16

Perform Basic File Editing Operations Using vi

This chapter provides information and commands concerning the following topics:

- Navigate a document using vi
- Use basic vi modes
- Insert, edit, delete, copy and find text
- vi
- /, ?
- **h, j, k ,l**
- **i, o, a**
- **c, d, p, y, dd, yy**
- **ZZ, :w!, :q!, :e!**

Navigate a Document Using vi

See the "h, j, k, l" section in this chapter for details.

Use Basic vi Modes

Because the vi editor was designed to only use a keyboard, this poses a challenge because sometimes a key should execute a command and sometimes a key should represent a character to insert into the document. To allow the keys to perform different tasks, vi has three modes of operation:

- **Command mode**—This mode is the default mode. When you open vi, you are placed in the command mode. Within this mode you can perform commands that can move around the screen, delete text, and paste text.

- **Insert mode**—While you're in insert mode, any key typed will appear in your document as new text. When you are finished adding new text, you can return to the default mode (the command mode) by pressing the Escape key. See "h, j, k, l" section in this chapter for details regarding how to get into the command mode.

- **Last line mode**—The last line mode, also called the *ex mode*, allows you to perform more complex operations, such as saving a document to a file with a different name. To enter into last line mode from the command mode, press the : key. After you enter your command and press Enter, the command is executed and normally you are returned to the command mode. In some cases, you may need to press the Escape key to return to the command mode. See the "ZZ, :w!, :q!, :e!" section in this chapter for examples of last line mode commands.

> **NOTE:** You cannot move from the insert mode to the last line mode, or vice versa. To move to the insert mode or the last line mode, you first must be in the command mode. Pressing the Escape key places you in the command mode.

Insert, Edit, Delete, Copy, and Find Text

See the following sections in this chapter for details:

- "/, ?"
- "i, o, a"
- "c, d, p, y, dd, yy"

vi

The vi editor is a standard text editor for both Linux and Unix environments. Although it may not be as user-friendly as other editors, it has a few important advantages:

- The vi editor (or vim, an improved version of the vi editor) is on every Linux distribution (and all Unix flavors). This means if you know how to edit files with the vi editor, you can always edit a file regardless of which distribution you are working on.

- Because the vi editor is a command-line only editor, it does not require a graphical user interface (GUI). This is important because many Linux servers do not have a GUI installed, which means you can't use GUI-based text editors.

- Once you understand vi very well, you will find it is a very efficient editor and you can edit files very quickly compared to most other editors. This is because all commands are short and keyboard-based, so you don't have to waste time taking your hands off of the keyboard to use the mouse.

To edit a new file with the vi editor, you can just type the command with no arguments or type **vi** *filename*.

A note about vim: The vim editor is an improved text editor that has additional features that are not found in the vi editor. Many Linux distributions use the vim editor by default. One advantage of the vim editor is that it includes all of the features and commands of the vi editor. So, if you learned the vi editor 30 years ago, then your knowledge would still apply when working in the vim editor. All of the commands in this chapter work in both editors.

/, ?

To search for files while in the vi editor, you can use either the / or ? character when you are working in the command mode. When you type either the / or ? character, you will see a prompt appear at the bottom-left side of the screen, as shown in Figure 16.1.

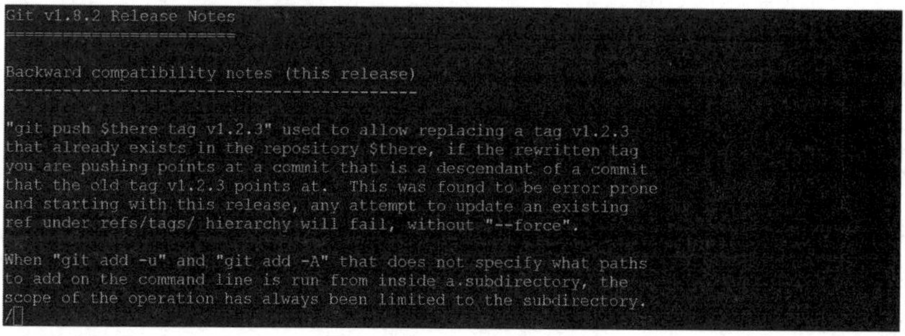

Figure 16.1   Searching for Files in the vi Editor

At the **/** or **?** prompt, type the value that you want to search for. You can use regular expressions within this value. For example, if you type **/^the**, then the vi editor will search for the next occurrence of the string "the" that appears at the beginning of a line.

The **/** character performs a forward search, and **?** searches backward in the document. If you don't find what you are searching for, you can use the **n** character to find the next match. When the search is started with a **/** character, the **n** character will continue the search forward in the document. When the search is started with a **?** character, the **n** character will continue the search backward in the document.

To reverse the current search, use the **N** character. For example, suppose you start the search by typing **?^the**. Using the **N** character would result in searching forward in the document.

h, j, k, l

While in the command mode, you can move around the screen by using the following keys:

Key	Description
h	Move one character to the left.
j	Move one line down.
k	Move one line up.
l	Move one character to the right.

i, o, a

While in the command mode, you can enter the insert mode by using one of the following keys:

Key	Description
i	Enter insert mode before the character the cursor is on; use the **I** key to insert before the beginning of the current line.
o	Open a new line below the current line and enter the insert mode; use the **O** key to open a line above the current line.
a	Enter insert mode after the character the cursor is on; use the **A** key to insert after the end of the current line.

c, d, p, y, dd, yy

While in the command mode, you can modify text by using the following keys:

Key	Description
c	Used to change text, the **c** key is combined with other keys to change data. For example, **cw** will change the current word and **c$** will change from the cursor position to the end of the line. When finished making your changes, press the Escape key.
d	Used to delete text, the **d** key is combined with other keys to delete data. For example, **dw** will delete the current word and **d$** will delete from the cursor position to the end of the line. All of the deleted data is stored in a buffer and can be pasted back into the document with the **p** or **P** key.
p	After cutting text with the **d** key or copying text with the **y** key, you can paste with the **p** or **P** key. A lowercase **p** will paste after the current cursor, whereas an uppercase **P** will paste before the cursor.
y	Used to copy text, the **y** key is combined with other keys to copy data. For example, **yw** will copy the current word and **y$** will copy from the cursor position to the end of the line. All of the copied data is stored in a buffer and can be pasted back into the document with the **p** or **P** key.
dd	The **dd** command will delete the current line.
yy	The **yy** command will copy the current line.

ZZ, :w!, :q!, :e!

While in the command mode, you can save and/or quit your document by entering the following keys:

Key	Description
ZZ	Saves and quits the document. This is equivalent to **:wq**.
:w!	Forces the vi editor to write changes in the document to the file.
:q!	Forces the vi editor to quit, even if changes in the file have not been saved.
:e!	Open a new file to edit and forget all changes in the document since the last write. This requires a filename argument as an option (for example, **:e! myfile.txt**).

CHAPTER 17

Create Partitions and Filesystems

This chapter provides information and commands concerning the following topics:

- Manage MBR partition tables
- Use various **mkfs** commands to create various filesystems, such as ext2/ext3/ext4, XFS, and VFAT
- Awareness of ReiserFS and btrfs
- Basic knowledge of **gdisk** and **parted** with GP
- **fdisk**
- **gdisk**
- **parted**
- **mkfs**
- **mkswap**

Manage MBR Partition Tables

MBR partition tables are often referred to as "traditional" partitions, as opposed to newer partition tables such as the GUID partition table. An MBR partition table has the restriction of only permitting four partitions by default. This is an extremely limiting factor for operating systems such as Linux.

However, one of the primary partitions in an MBR partition table can be converted into an extended partition. Within this extended partition, additional partitions can be added. These additional partitions are called *logical* partitions. See Figure 17.1 for a visual example.

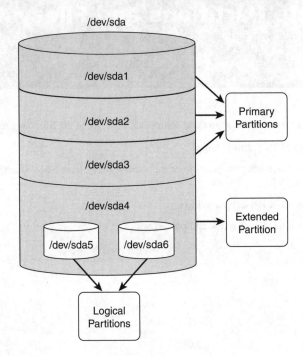

Figure 17.1   Partitions

See the "fdisk" and "parted" sections in this chapter for details on creating MBR partitions.

A note regarding hard disk device names: Hard disks are referred to via devices names in the **/dev** directory. IDE-based devices have names that start with **/dev/hd**, whereas SETA, SCSI, and USB devices have names that start with **/dev/sd**. The first drive on the system is named **a**, so the first SETA device would be **/dev/sda**. The second SETA would be **/dev/sdb**, and so on. Partitions are numbered sequentially, starting from 1, such as **/dev/sda1**, **/dev/sda2**, and **/dev/sda3**.

Use Various mkfs Commands to Create Various Filesystems, Such As ext2/ext3/ext4, XFS, and VFAT

See the "mkfs" section in this chapter for details.

Awareness of ReiserFS and btrfs

The LPIC-101 exam may have some theory-based questions regarding ReiserFS and btrfs—two alternate Linux filesystems. These filesystems are at opposite ends of their lifecycles, as btrfs use has recently become more widespread while ReiserFS's popularity has diminished (due largely to the fact that the sole maintainer of the code is no longer available to provide updates).

ReiserFS is a journal filesystem and was known for good performance on filesystems that had many small files.

The btrfs filesystem uses copy-on-write (CoW) and other advanced filesystem features.

Basic Knowledge of gdisk and parted with GP

See the "gdisk" and "parted" sections in this chapter for details.

fdisk

The **fdisk** utility is an interactive tool that allows you to display and modify traditional (non-GUID) partition tables. To display a partition table, use the **-l** option (as the root user), like so:

```
[root@localhost ~]$ fdisk -l /dev/sda
```

```
Disk /dev/sda: 42.9 GB, 42949672960 bytes
4 heads, 32 sectors/track, 655360 cylinders, total 83886080 sectors
Units = sectors of 1 * 512 = 512 bytes
Sector size (logical/physical): 512 bytes / 512 bytes
I/O size (minimum/optimal): 512 bytes / 512 bytes
Disk identifier: 0x000c566f
```

```
   Device Boot      Start         End      Blocks   Id  System
/dev/sda1   *        2048    83886079    41942016   83  Linux
```

To modify the partition table of a drive, run the **fdisk** command without the **-l** option:

```
[root@localhost ~]$ fdisk -l /dev/sda
Command (m for help):
```

There are several useful commands you can type at the "Command" prompt, including the following:

Command	Description
d	Delete a partition.
l	List partition types.
m	Print a menu of possible commands.
n	Create a new partition.
p	Print the current partition table.
q	Quit without saving any changes.
t	Change a partition table type.
w	Write (save) changes to the partition table on the hard drive.

gdisk

The **gdisk** utility is an interactive tool that allows you to display and modify GUID partition tables. If executed on a device that contains a non-GUID partition table, such as a traditional MBR table, the **gdisk** command will convert the table to GUID format.

To display a partition table, use the **-l** option (run this command as the root user):

```
[root@localhost ~]$ gdisk -l /dev/sda
GPT fdisk (gdisk) version 0.8.8


Partition table scan:
  MBR: MBR only
  BSD: not present
  APM: not present
  GPT: not present


******************************************************************
Found invalid GPT and valid MBR; converting MBR to GPT format
in memory.
******************************************************************

Warning! Secondary partition table overlaps the last partition by
33 blocks!
You will need to delete this partition or resize it in another
utility.
Disk /dev/sda: 83886080 sectors, 40.0 GiB
Logical sector size: 512 bytes
Disk identifier (GUID): 9D81DAEA-CC37-46CB-8E17-C54626E9AD8D
Partition table holds up to 128 entries
First usable sector is 34, last usable sector is 83886046
Partitions will be aligned on 2048-sector boundaries
Total free space is 2014 sectors (1007.0 KiB)


Number  Start (sector)   End (sector)  Size      Code   Name
   1          2048         83886079   40.0 GiB   8300   Linux filesystem
```

To modify the partition table of a drive, run the **gdisk** command without the **-l** option:

```
[root@localhost ~]$ gdisk/dev/sda
GPT fdisk (gdisk) version 0.8.8


Command (? for help):
```

There are several useful commands you can type at the "Command" prompt, including the following:

Command	Description
d	Delete a partition.
i	Display details about a partition.
l	List partition types.
?	Print a menu of possible commands.
n	Create a new partition.
p	Print the current partition table.
q	Quit without saving any changes.
t	Change a partition table type.
w	Write (save) changes to the partition table on the hard drive.

parted

The **parted** utility is an interactive tool that allows you to display and modify both traditional and GUID partition tables. It can also create a filesystem on a partition.

To display a partition table, use the **-l** option (run this command as the root user):

```
[root@localhost ~]$ parted -l /dev/sda
Model: ATA VBOX HARDDISK (scsi)
Disk /dev/sda: 42.9GB
Sector size (logical/physical): 512B/512B
Partition Table: msdos


Number  Start    End     Size    Type     File system  Flags
 1      1049kB   42.9GB  42.9GB  primary  ext4         boot


Model: Linux device-mapper (thin) (dm)
Disk /dev/mapper/docker-8:1-264916-
f9bd50927a44b83330c036684911b54e494e4e48efbc2329262b6f0e909e3d7d: 107GB
Sector size (logical/physical): 512B/512B
Partition Table: loop


Number  Start    End     Size    File system  Flags
 1      0.00B    107GB   107GB   ext4
```

```
Model: Linux device-mapper (thin) (dm)
Disk /dev/mapper/docker-8:1-264916-
77a4c5c2f607aa6b31a37280ac39a657bfd7ece1d940e50507fb0c128c220f7a: 107GB
Sector size (logical/physical): 512B/512B
Partition Table: loop

Number   Start    End    Size    File system  Flags
 1       0.00B    107GB  107GB   ext4
```

To modify the partition table of a drive, run the **parted** command without the **-l** option:

```
[root@localhost ~]$ parted/dev/sda
GNU Parted 2.3
Using /dev/sda
Welcome to GNU Parted! Type 'help' to view a list of commands.
(parted)
```

There are several useful commands you can type at the "parted" prompt, including the following:

Command	Description
rm	Delete a partition.
? or help	Print a menu of possible commands.
mkpart	Create a new partition.
mkpartfs	Create a new partition and filesystem.
print	Print the current partition table.
quit	Quit without saving any changes.
w	Write (save) changes to the partition table on the hard drive.

mkfs

The **mkfs** command will create a filesystem on a partition. The basic syntax of the command is **mkfs -t** *fstype partition*. The *fstype* can be one of the following:

Type	Description
ext2	Create an ext2 filesystem (the default on most distributions).
ext3	Create an ext3 filesystem.
ext4	Create an ext4 filesystem.
bfs	Create a btrfs filesystem.
vfat	Create a VFAT (DOS) filesystem.
ntfs	Create an NTFS (Windows) filesystem.
xfs	Create an XFS filesystem.

Note that the **mkfs** command is a front-end utility to other commands. For example, executing the command **mkfs -t ext4 /dev/sdb7** will result in the **mkfs.ext4 /dev/sdb7** command being executed.

Each specific filesystem-creation utility has dozens of possible options that affect how the filesystem is created. These options are passed from the **mkfs** command to the specific filesystem-creation command that **mkfs** launches.

mkswap

The **mkswap** command will convert a partition or a file into a device that can be used as virtual memory. For example, to create a swap file, first create a large file with the **dd** command (see the "dd" section in Chapter 11, "Perform Basic File Management," for details regarding the **dd** command). Then convert it with the **mkswap** command (run these commands as the root user):

```
[root@localhost ~]$ dd if=/dev/zero of=/var/extraswap count=30 bs=1M
30+0 records in
30+0 records out
31457280 bytes (31 MB) copied, 0.0153054 s, 2.1 GB/s
[root@localhost ~]$ mkswap /var/extraswap
Setting up swapspace version 1, size = 30716 KiB
no label, UUID=4865b474-2219-4fca-a689-6d680024c0fe
```

swapon

The **swapon** command will take a valid swap device and enable it to be used as virtual memory on the system. To add a swap file to virtual memory, execute the **swapon** command with the **-a** option (run these commands as the root user):

```
[root@localhost ~]$ swapon -s
Filename                        Type        Size     Used     Priority
/dev/sda2                       partition   124048   0        -1
[root@localhost ~]$ swapon -a /var/extraswap
[root@localhost ~]$ swapon -s
Filename                        Type        Size     Used     Priority
/dev/sda2                       partition   124048   0        -1
/var/extraswap                  file        30716    0        -1
```

To remove a swap device from virtual memory, use the **-d** option to the **swapon** command: **swapon –d /var/extraswap.**

Using the **swapon** command results in a temporary change; after a system reboot, the swap device will not be used as virtual memory unless it is added to the **/etc/fstab** file as shown:

```
/var/extraswap   swap          swap defaults            0 0
```

## CHAPTER 18

Maintain the Integrity of Filesystems

This chapter provides information and commands concerning the following topics:

- Verify the integrity of filesystems
- Monitor free space and inodes
- Repair simple filesystem problems
- **du**
- **df**
- **fsck**
- **e2fsck**
- **mke2fs**
- **debugfs**
- **dumpe2fs**
- **tune2fs**
- XFS tools (such as **xfs_metadump** and **xfs_info**)

Verify the Integrity of Filesystems

See the "tune2fs," "dumpe2fs," and "XFS Tools" sections in this chapter for details.

Monitor Free Space and Inodes

See the "du" and "df" sections in this chapter for details.

Repair Simple Filesystem Problems

See the "fsck" and "e2fsck" sections in this chapter for details.

du

The **du** command provides an estimated amount of disk space usage in a directory structure. For example, the following command displays the amount of space used in the **/usr/lib** directory:

```
[root@localhost ~]$ du -sh /usr/lib
791M    /usr/lib
```

Important options for the **du** command include the following:

Option	Description
-h	Display values in a human-readable size (instead of always displaying in bytes, it will display in more understandable values, such as megabytes or kilobytes, depending on the overall size of the file).
-s	Display a summary, rather than the size of each subdirectory.

df

The **df** command displays usage of partitions and logical devices:

```
[root@localhost ~]$ df
Filesystem          1K-blocks     Used  Available  Use%  Mounted on
udev                  2019204       12    2019192    1%  /dev
tmpfs                  404832      412     404420    1%  /run
/dev/sda1            41251136  6992272   32522952   18%  /
none                        4        0          4    0%  /sys/fs/cgroup
none                     5120        0       5120    0%  /run/lock
none                  2024144        0    2024144    0%  /run/shm
none                   102400        0     102400    0%  /run/user
```

Important options for the **df** command include the following:

Option	Description
-h	Display values in human-readable size.
-i	Display inode information.

fsck

The **fsck** utility is designed to find filesystem problems on unmounted filesystems (run this command as the root user):

```
[root@localhost ~]$ fsck /dev/sdb1
fsck from util-linux 2.20.1
e2fsck 1.42.9 (4-Feb-2014)
Pass 1: Checking inodes, blocks, and sizes
Pass 2: Checking directory structure
Pass 3: Checking directory connectivity
Pass 4: Checking reference counts
Pass 5: Checking group summary information
/dev/sdb1: 11/12544 files (0.0% non-contiguous), 6498/50176 blocks
```

This utility is fairly straightforward. It calls the correct filesystem check utility based on a probe of the filesystem and then prompts the user when errors are found. To fix an error, answer "y" or "yes" to the prompts.

Since "yes" is almost always the appropriate answer, the **fsck** utility supports a **-y** option, which automatically answers "yes" to each prompt.

e2fsck

The **fsck** command executes filesystem-specific utilities. In the case of ext2/ext3/ext4 filesystems, the **fsck** command executes the **e2fsck** utility. See the fsck section in this chapter for details regarding the **fsck** command.

mke2fs

The **mke2fs** command is designed specifically to create ext2/ext3/ext4 filesystems. It has more command-line options than the **mkfs** command. (See the "mkfs" section in Chapter 17, "Create Partitions and Filesystems," for details regarding the **mkfs** command.)

Important options for the **mke2fs** command include the following:

Option	Description
-b	Specify the block size.
-c	Check the filesystem for bad blocks.
-i	Specify the byte-to-inode ratio to determine how many inodes to create.
-j	Create a journal filesystem.
-L	Specify a filesystem label.
-m	Reserve a specific percentage of the filesystem for the system administrator.
-t	Specify the filesystem type (ext2, ext3, or ext4).

debugfs

The **debugfs** command allows you to interact with the filesystem directly rather than OS commands. To start the utility, pass an argument of a partition that contains a filesystem (run this command as the root user):

```
[root@localhost ~]$ debugfs /dev/sda1
debugfs 1.42.9 (4-Feb-2014)
debugfs:
```

When at the "debugfs": prompt, you have several commands available, including the following:

Command	Description
freefrag	Report free fragment space.
features	Display superblock features.
cd	Change working directory.

Command	Description
ls	List current directory contents.
mkdir	Make a directory.
rmdir	Remove a directory.
rm	Delete a file.
undel	Undelete a file.
quit	Quit the utility.

dumpe2fs

The **dumpe2fs** command will display filesystem metadata, as described in the following command:

```
[root@localhost ~]$ dumpe2fs /dev/sdb1 | head
dumpe2fs 1.42.9 (4-Feb-2014)
Filesystem volume name:   <none>
Last mounted on:          <not available>
Filesystem UUID:          dbc79125-2d95-47c7-8799-2ef7842c79cc
Filesystem magic number:  0xEF53
Filesystem revision #:    1 (dynamic)
Filesystem features:      has_journal ext_attr resize_inode dir_index
filetype sparse_super
Filesystem flags:         signed_directory_hash
Default mount options:    user_xattr acl
Filesystem state:         clean
Errors behavior:          Continue
```

NOTE: The previous command should be executed as the root user. Because the output of this command could be over 100 lines long, the **head** command was used to limit the output.

Although the **dump2efs** command has a few options, they are typically only employed in specific use cases.

tune2fs

The **tune2fs** command is used to display or modify specific metadata for an ext2/ext3/ext4 filesystem. For example, by default, 5% of an ext2/ext3/ext4 filesystem is reserved for the system administrator (run the following command as the root user):

```
[root@localhost ~]$ tune2fs -l /dev/sdb1 | grep block
Inode count:             12544
Block count:             50176
Reserved block count:    2508
Mount count:             0
Maximum mount count:     -1
```

Note that the reserved block count (2508) is 5% of the block count (50176). Use the following command to change this to a different percentage:

```
[root@localhost ~]$ tune2fs -m 20 /dev/sdb1
tune2fs 1.42.9 (4-Feb-2014)
Setting reserved blocks percentage to 20% (10035 blocks)
```

Important options for the **tune2fs** command include the following:

Option	Description
-J	Modify journal options.
-o	Modify mount options.
-L	Modify the filesystem label.
-l	List filesystem metadata.
-m	Modify the percentage of the filesystem reserved for the root user.

XFS Tools (Such As xfs_metadump and xfs_info)

The **xfs_metadump** command dumps (copies) metadata from an unmounted XFS filesystem into a file to be used for debugging purposes. Important options for XFS tools include the following:

Option	Description
-e	Stop the dump if a filesystem error if found.
-g	Show the progress of the dump.
-w	Display error messages if filesystem errors are found.

The **xfs_info** command is used to display the geometry of an XFS filesystem, similar to the **dumpe2fs** command for ext2/ext3/ext4 filesystems. There are no special options for the **xfs_info** command.

## CHAPTER 19

Control Mounting and Unmounting of Filesystems

This chapter provides information and commands concerning the following topics:

- Manually mount and unmount filesystems
- Configure filesystem mounting on bootup
- Configure user-mountable removable filesystems
- **/etc/fstab**
- **/media**
- **mount**
- **umount**

Manually Mount and Unmount Filesystems

See the "mount" and "umount" sections in this chapter for details.

Configure Filesystem Mounting on Bootup

See the "/etc/fstab" section in this chapter for details.

Configure User-Mountable Removable Filesystems

See the "/media" section in this chapter for details.

/etc/fstab

The **/etc/fstab** file is used to specify which filesystems to mount, where to mount the filesystems, and what options to use during the mount process. This file is used during the boot process to configure filesystems to mount on bootup.

Each line describes one mount process. The following is an example of one of these lines:

```
/dev/sda1       /                     ext4    defaults           1    1
```

Each line is broken into six fields of data, separated by whitespace:

- The device to mount (**/dev/sda1**).
- The mount point (**/**).
- The filesystem type (**ext4**).

- The mount options (**defaults**).

- Dump level (**1**). This field is related to the **dump** command and is rarely used.

- The **fsck** pass field (**1**). A value of 0 means "do not run **fsck** on this filesystem during system boot," whereas a value of 1 or higher means "run **fsck** on this filesystem during system boot."

/media

When removable media, such as CD-ROMs or DVDs, are automatically mounted, they are typically made available under the **/media** directory. There is no need to configure this process on a modern Linux distribution that is using a GUI, such as Gnome or KDE, as these software programs recognize new removable media and automatically mount.

However, on a system that does not have a running GUI, this automatic mount process does not take place. You can configure the system so a regular user can mount a removable device by using the following **/etc/fstab** entry:

```
/dev/cdrom /media udf,iso9660 noauto,owner 0 0
```

See the "/etc/fstab" section in this chapter for additional details regarding the **/etc/fstab** file.

mount

The **mount** command can display the currently mounted filesystems:

```
[root@localhost ~]$ mount
/dev/sda1 on / type ext4 (rw)
proc on /proc type proc (rw,noexec,nosuid,nodev)
sysfs on /sys type sysfs (rw,noexec,nosuid,nodev)
none on /sys/fs/cgroup type tmpfs (rw)
none on /sys/fs/fuse/connections type fusectl (rw)
none on /sys/kernel/debug type debugfs (rw)
none on /sys/kernel/security type securityfs (rw)
udev on /dev type devtmpfs (rw,mode=0755)
devpts on /dev/pts type devpts (rw,noexec,nosuid,gid=5,mode=0620)
tmpfs on /run type tmpfs (rw,noexec,nosuid,size=10%,mode=0755)
none on /run/lock type tmpfs (rw,noexec,nosuid,nodev,size=5242880)
none on /run/shm type tmpfs (rw,nosuid,nodev)
none on /run/user type tmpfs (rw,noexec,nosuid,nodev,size=104857600,
mode=0755)
none on /sys/fs/pstore type pstore (rw)
rpc_pipefs on /run/rpc_pipefs type rpc_pipefs (rw)
systemd on /sys/fs/cgroup/systemd type cgroup (rw,noexec,nosuid,nodev,
none,name=systemd)
```

The **mount** command can also be used to manually mount a filesystem. Provide the device to mount as the first argument and the mount point (mount directory) as the second argument (execute the following commands as the root user):

```
[root@localhost ~]$ mkdir /data
[root@localhost ~]$ mount /dev/sdb1 /data
```

Important options for the **mount** command include the following:

Option	Description
-a	Mount all filesystems listed in the **/etc/fstab** file that have a mount option of "auto."
-o	Specify a mount option (for example, **mount -o acl /dev/sdb1 / data**).
-t	Specify the filesystem type to mount. This is typically not necessary because the **mount** command can determine the filesystem type by probing the partition.

umount

Use the **umount** command to manually unmount a filesystem:

```
[root@localhost ~]$ mount | grep /data
/dev/sdb1 on /data type ext3 (rw)
[root@localhost ~]$ umount /data
```

Important options for the **umount** command include the following:

Option	Description
-r	Attempt to mount the filesystem as read-only if the unmount operation fails.
-f	Force the unmount. This is typically used on NFS mounts when the NFS server is nonresponsive.

## CHAPTER 20

Manage Disk Quotas

This chapter provides information and commands concerning the following topics:

- Set up a disk quota for a filesystem
- Edit, check, and generate user quota reports
- **quota**
- **edquota**
- **repquota**
- **quotaon**

Set Up a Disk Quota for a Filesystem

To enable user quotas, you must mount the filesystem with the **usrquota** mount option. This can be accomplished by adding **usrquota** to the mount option field of the **/etc/fstab** file:

```
/dev/sdb1        /                  ext4    usrquota            1   1
```

Then you can remount the filesystem with the following command (executed by the root user):

```
[root@localhost ~]$ mount -o remount /
```

See the "/etc/fstab" and "mount" sections in Chapter 19, "Control Mounting and Unmounting of Filesystems," for additional details regarding these tasks.

After mounting the filesystem with the **usrquota** option enabled, you need to create the initial quota databases by executing the following **quotacheck** command:

```
[root@localhost ~]$ quotacheck -cugm /dev/sdb1
```

This will result in new files in the mount point directory of the filesystem:

```
[root@localhost ~]$ ls /aquota*
/aquota.group   /aquota.user
```

Important options for the **quotacheck** command include the following:

Option	Description
-c	Create database file(s).
-g	Only create the **aquota.group** file, which means only group quotas will be enabled unless the **-u** option is also used.
-m	Do not attempt to unmount the filesystem while creating the quota file(s).
-u	Only create the **aquota.user** file, which means only user quotas will be enabled unless the **-g** option is also used.

Edit, Check, and Generate User Quota Reports

After setting up disk quotas, as described in the "Set Up a Disk Quota for a Filesystem" section of this chapter, follow these steps to enable and display quotas for users:

1. Turn on disk quotas by executing the **quotaon** command. (See the "quotaon" section in this chapter for details.)

2. Create or edit a user quota by using the **edquota** command. (See the "edquota" section in this chapter for details.)

3. Display quota information by using the **quota** or **repquota** command. (See the "quota" and "repquota" sections in this chapter for details.)

quota

The **quota** command can be executed by a user to display the quotas for the account:

```
[sarah@localhost ~]$ quota
Disk quotas for user sarah (uid 507):
    Filesystem  blocks   quota   limit   grace   files   quota   limit   grace
    /dev/sda1    20480   30000   60000               1       0       0
```

Note the output when a user has exceeded a soft quota; in the following example, the user sarah is above the soft limit for block size:

```
[sarah@localhost ~]$ quota
Disk quotas for user sarah (uid 507):
    Filesystem  blocks   quota   limit   grace   files   quota   limit   grace
    /dev/sda1   40960*   30000   60000   7days       2       0       0
```

Once the user has exceeded a soft quota, a grace period is provided. The user must reduce the space used in the filesystem to be below the soft quota within the grace period or else the current usage converts to a hard quota limit.

NOTE: The grace period can be set by the root user by executing the **edquota -t** command. See the "edquota" section for more details that command.

Important options for the **quota** command include the following:

Option	Description
-g	Display group quotas instead of specific user quotas.
-s	Display information in human-readable sizes rather than block sizes.
-l	Display quota information only for local filesystems (rather than network-based filesystem quotas).

edquota

To create or edit a user's quotas, execute the **edquota** command followed by the username (the following command must be executed by the root user):

```
[root@localhost ~]$ edquota sarah
```

The **edquota** command will enter an editor (vi is typically the default) and display all of the user's quotas. The output will look something like the following:

```
Disk quotas for user sarah (uid 507):
    Filesystem   blocks    soft    hard    inodes    soft    hard
    /dev/sdb1    550060       0       0     29905       0       0
```

The following table describes the fields of the quota:

Key	Description
Filesystem	The partition that contains the filesystem with quotas enabled.
blocks	How many blocks the user currently uses in the filesystem.
soft	A value that represents a soft quota for blocks; if the user creates a file that results in exceeding this block limit, a warning is issued.
hard	A value that represents a hard quota for blocks; if the user creates a file that results in exceeding this block limit, an error is issued and no additional files can be created in the filesystem.
inodes	How many files the user currently has in the filesystem.
soft	A value that represents a soft quota for files; if the user creates a file that results in exceeding this file limit, a warning is issued.
hard	A value that represents a hard quota for file; if the user creates a file that results in exceeding this file limit, an error is issued and no additional files can be created in the filesystem.

NOTE: The grace period can be set by executing the **edquota -t** command. See the "quota" section for more details regarding the grace period.

repquota

The **repquota** command is used by the root user to display quotas for an entire filesystem (the following command must be executed by the root user):

```
[root@localhost ~]$ repquota /
*** Report for user quotas on device /dev/sda1
Block grace time: 7days; Inode grace time: 7days
                        Block limits              File limits
User             used    soft    hard   grace   used   soft   hard   grace
----------------------------------------------------------------------------
root        --  4559956     0       0          207396    0     0
daemon      --       64     0       0               4    0     0
man         --     1832     0       0             145    0     0
www-data    --        4     0       0               1    0     0
libuuid     --       40     0       0               6    0     0
syslog      --     3848     0       0              23    0     0
messagebus  --        8     0       0               2    0     0
landscape   --        8     0       0               2    0     0
pollinate   --        4     0       0               1    0     0
vagrant     --   550060     0       0           29906    0     0
colord      --        8     0       0               2    0     0
statd       --       12     0       0               3    0     0
puppet      --       44     0       0              11    0     0
ubuntu      --       36     0       0               8    0     0
sarah       +-    40960  30000   60000   6days       2    0     0
```

Important options for the **repquota** command include the following:

Option	Description
-a	Display quotas for all filesystems with quota mount options specified in the **/etc/fstab** file.
-g	Display group quotas instead of specific user quotas.
-s	Display information in human-readable sizes rather than block sizes.

quotaon

The **quotaon** command is used to turn quotas on for a filesystem. Normally when the system is booted, it will turn on quotas automatically. However, you may turn off quotas by executing the **quotaoff** command followed by the name of the filesystem (the following commands must be executed by the root user):

```
[root@localhost ~]$ quotaoff /dev/sdb1
[root@localhost ~]$ quotaon /dev/sdb1
```

## CHAPTER 21

Manage File Permissions and Ownership

This chapter provides information and commands concerning the following topics:

- Manage access permissions on regular and special files as well as directories
- Use access modes such as **suid**, **sgid**, and the sticky bit to maintain security
- Know how to change the file creation mask
- Use the group field to grant file access to group members
- **chmod**
- **umask**
- **chown**
- **chgrp**

Manage Access Permissions on Regular and Special Files As Well As Directories

See the "chmod" section in this chapter for details.

Use Access Modes Such As suid, sgid, and the Sticky Bit to Maintain Security

The following table describes the special permission sets of **suid**, **sgid**, and the sticky bit:

	suid	sgid	Sticky Bit
Description	When set on executable files, suid allows a program to access files using the permissions of the user owner of the executable file.	When set on executable files, sgid allows a program to access files using the permissions of the group owner of the executable file. When it's set on directories, all new files in the directory inherit the group ownership of the directory.	When the sticky bit is set on directories, files in the directory can only be removed by the user owner of the file, the owner of the directory, or the root user.

	suid	sgid	Sticky Bit
Set	chmod u+s file or chmod 1*xxx* file (*xxx* refers to regular read, write, and execute permissions.)	chmod g+s file or chmod 2*xxx* file (*xxx* refers to regular read, write, and execute permissions.)	chmod o+t file or chmod 4*xxx* file (*xxx* refers to regular read, write, and execute permissions.) Note: Sticky bit permissions are almost always set to the octal value of 1777.
Remove	chmod u-s file or chmod 0*xxx* file	chmod g-s file or chmod 0*xxx* file	chmod o-t file or chmod 0*xxx* file

See the "chmod" section in this chapter for details about the **chmod** command.

Know How to Change the File Creation Mask

See the "umask" section in this chapter for details.

Use the Group Field to Grant File Access to Group Members

To grant access to a file for specific members of a group, change the group ownership of the file by using either the **chown** or **chgrp** command. See the "chown" and "chgrp" sections in this chapter for details.

chmod

Use the **chmod** command to modify permissions on a file or directory. The format of the command is **chmod [options]** *permission_set file|directory*.

The permission_set can be either symbolic or octal (also called *numeric*). The symbolic method only changes specific permissions, whereas the octal method is used to change all permissions for the file or directory.

To set permissions using the symbolic method, use the following values for the *permission_set*:

Who:

- **u** = user owner
- **g** = group owner

- **o** = other
- **a** = all three permission sets

Add or remove:

- **+** = add
- **–** = remove

Permission:

- **r** = read
- **w** = write
- **x** = execute

The following table demonstrates some examples using the symbolic method:

Example	Description
chmod u+r file	Add read permission for the user owner.
chmod ug-w file	Remove write permission for the user owner and group owner.
chmod a+r file	Add read permission to all permission sets.
chmod go+rw file	Remove read and write permissions to the group owner and others.
chmod u+r,g-w file	Add read permission for the user owner and remove write permission for the group owner.

With the octal method, values are assigned to the permissions of read, write and execute:

- read = **4**
- write = **2**
- execute = **1**

As a result, any possible combination of read, write, and execute can be specified with a single numeric value between 0 and 7:

- **7** = read (**4**), write (**2**) and execute (**1**)
- **6** = read and write
- **5** = read and execute
- **4** = read
- **3** = write and execute
- **2** = write
- **1** = execute
- **0** = no permission set

The following table demonstrates some examples using the octal method:

Example	Description
chmod 755 file	Sets the permissions of rwxr-xr-x.
chmod 511 file	Sets the permissions of r-x--x--x.
chmod 600 file	Sets the permissions of rw-------.

Important options for the **chmod** command include the following:

Option	Description
-R	Recursively apply changes to an entire directory structure.
-v	Verbose. Produce output demonstrating the changes that are made.

umask

The **umask** command sets default permissions for files and directories. These default permissions are applied only when the file or directory is initially created.

The **umask** command accepts one argument: the mask value. The mask value is an octal value that is applied against the maximum possible permissions for new files or new directories, as shown in the following table:

Type	Maximum Possible Permission for New Item
File	rw-rw-rw-
Directory	rwxrwxrwx

Figure 21.1 describes how a umask value of **027** would apply to new files versus how it would apply to new directories.

Description	File			Directories		
Maximum	rw-	rw-	rw-	rwx	rwx	rwx
Umask Applied	---	-M-	MM-	---	-M-	MM-
Result	rw-	r--	---	rwx	r-x	--x

Figure 21.1   How umask is applied

NOTE: Each shell has its own umask value. If you change the umask in one shell, it will not affect the umask value in any other shell. To make a persistent change to your umask across logins, add the **umask** command to the **~/.bash_profile** file.

chown

The **chown** command is used to change the user owner or group owner of a file or directory. The following table demonstrates different ways to use this command:

Example	Description
chown tim abc.txt	Changes the user owner of the **abc.txt** file to tim user.
chown tim:staff abc.txt	Changes the user owner of the **abc.txt** file to tim user and the group owner to the staff group.
chown :staff abc.txt	Changes the group owner of the **abc.txt** file to the staff group.

NOTE: Only the root user can change the user owner of a file. To change the group owner of a file, the user who executes the command must own the file and be a member of the group that the ownership is being changed to.

Important options for the **chown** command include the following:

Option	Description
-R	Recursively apply changes to an entire directory structure.
--reference=*file*	Change the user and group owner to the ownership of *file*.
-v	Verbose. Produce output demonstrating the changes that are made.

chgrp

The **chgrp** command is designed to change the group ownership of a file. The syntax of this command is **chgrp** [*options*] *group_name file*. In the following example, the group ownership of the **abc.txt** file is changed to the staff group:

```
[student@localhost ~]$ chgrp staff abc.txt
```

NOTE: To change the group owner of a file, the user who executes the command must own the file and be a member of the group that the ownership is being changed to.

Important options for the **chgrp** command include the following:

Option	Description
-R	Recursively apply changes to an entire directory structure.
--reference=*file*	Change the user and group owner to the ownership of *file*.
-v	Verbose. Produce output demonstrating the changes that are made.

## CHAPTER 22

Create and Change Hard and Symbolic Links

This chapter provides information and commands concerning the following topics:

- Create links
- Identify hard and/or soft links
- Copying versus linking files
- Use links to support system administration tasks
- **ln**
- **ls**

Create Links

See the "ln" section in this chapter for details.

Identify Hard and/or Soft Links

See the "ls" section in this chapter for details.

Copying Versus Linking Files

There are two different types of link files: hard links and soft (also called symbolic) links. Understanding these link types is important when determining if you should link a file or make a file copy.

Hard Links

When you create a hard link to a file, there is no way to distinguish the "original" file versus the "linked" file. They are just two filenames that point to the same inode, and hence the same data. If you have 10 hard-linked files and you delete any nine of these files, the data is still maintained in the remaining file.

Figure 22.1 demonstrates hard links.

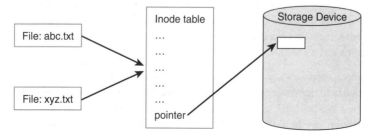

Figure 22.1   Hard Links

In Figure 22.1, the **abc.txt** and **xyz.txt** files are hard-linked together. This means that they share the same inode tables. The "…" in the inode table represents metadata—information about the file such as the user owner and permissions. Included with this metadata are pointers that refer to blocks within the storage device where the file data is stored.

Soft Links

When you create a soft link, the original file contains the data while the link file "points to" the original file. Any changes made to the original will also appear to be in the linked file because using the linked file always results in following the link to the target file. Deleting the original file results in a broken link, making the link file worthless and resulting in complete data loss.

Figure 22.2 demonstrates soft links.

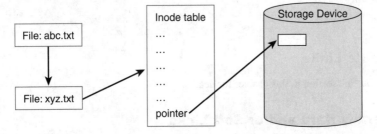

Figure 22.2   Soft Links

In Figure 22.2, the **abc.txt** file is soft linked to the xyz.txt file. The **abc.txt** file points to the filename **xyz.txt**, not the same inode table (although not shown in this figure, the **abc.txt** file has its own inode table). When the process that is accessing the link file follows the link, the data for the **xyz.txt** file is accessible via the **abc.txt** file.

Copying files results in a complete and separate copy of the data. Changes in the original file have no effect on the data in the copied file. Changes in the copied file have no effect on the data in the original file. Deleting one of these files has no impact on the other file.

Use Links to Support System Administration Tasks

The primary use of links for system administration tasks is when an administrator decides to move the location of a key file to a different directory location (or give the file a different name). This can cause some confusion for users who are used to the original file location and name.

For example, suppose a key configuration file is named **/etc/setup-db.conf** and the administrator wants to move this file into the **/etc/db** directory. After moving the file, the admin can create a symbolic link to help other users (and perhaps programs) to find the correct data, as shown here (note that the following command must be run as the root user):

```
[root@localhost ~]$ ln -s /etc/db/setup-db.conf /etc/setup-db.conf
```

The **/etc** directory has several examples of this use of links:

```
[root@localhost ~]$ ls -l /etc | grep "^l"
lrwxrwxrwx   1 root root        12 Jan 26   2015 drupal -> /etc/drupal6
lrwxrwxrwx   1 root root        56 Dec 17   2013 favicon.png ->
/usr/share/icons/hicolor/16x16/apps/fedora-logo-icon.png
lrwxrwxrwx   1 root root        22 Jan 23   2015 grub2.cfg ->
../boot/grub2/grub.cfg
lrwxrwxrwx   1 root root        22 Dec 17   2013 grub.conf ->
../boot/grub/grub.conf
lrwxrwxrwx   1 root root        11 Jan 23   2015 init.d -> rc.d/init.d
lrwxrwxrwx   1 root root        41 Feb 18   2015 localtime ->
../usr/share/zoneinfo/America/Los_Angeles
lrwxrwxrwx   1 root root        12 Dec 17   2013 mtab -> /proc/mounts
lrwxrwxrwx   1 root root        10 Jan 23   2015 rc0.d -> rc.d/rc0.d
lrwxrwxrwx   1 root root        10 Jan 23   2015 rc1.d -> rc.d/rc1.d
lrwxrwxrwx   1 root root        10 Jan 23   2015 rc2.d -> rc.d/rc2.d
lrwxrwxrwx   1 root root        10 Jan 23   2015 rc3.d -> rc.d/rc3.d
lrwxrwxrwx   1 root root        10 Jan 23   2015 rc4.d -> rc.d/rc4.d
lrwxrwxrwx   1 root root        10 Jan 23   2015 rc5.d -> rc.d/rc5.d
lrwxrwxrwx   1 root root        10 Jan 23   2015 rc6.d -> rc.d/rc6.d
lrwxrwxrwx   1 root root        14 Sep 10 12:58 redhat-release ->
fedora-release
lrwxrwxrwx   1 root root        14 Sep 10 12:58 system-release ->
fedora-release
```

ln

To create a link, execute the **ln** command in the following manner: **ln [-s]** *target_file*
link_file. For example, to create a hard link from the **/etc/hosts** file to a file in the current
directory called **myhosts**, execute the following command:

```
[root@localhost ~]$ ln /etc/hosts myhosts
```

Hard-linked files share the same inode. You can only make a hard link to a file (not a
directory) that resides on the same filesystem as the original file. Creating hard links to
files on another filesystem or to directories will result in errors:

```
[root@localhost ~]$ ln /boot/initrd.img-3.16.0-30-generic initrd
ln: failed to create hard link 'initrd' => '/boot/initrd.img-3.16.
0-30-generic': Invalid cross-device link
[root@localhost ~]$ ln /etc myetc
ln: '/etc': hard link not allowed for directory
```

Soft links (also called *symbolic links*) are files that point to other files (or directories) via
the filesystem. You can create a soft link to any file or directory:

```
[root@localhost ~]$ ln -s /boot/initrd.img-3.16.0-30-generic initrd
```

See the "ls" section in this chapter to learn how to view existing link files.

ls

The **ls** command can be used to view both soft and hard links. Soft links are very easy to see because the target file is displayed when executing the **ls -l** command:

```
[root@localhost ~]$ ls -l /etc/vtrgb
lrwxrwxrwx 1 root root 23 Jul 11  2015 /etc/vtrgb -> /etc/alterna-
tives/vtrgb
```

Hard links are more difficult because a hard link file shares an inode with another file-name. For example, the value 2 after the permissions in the following output indicates this is a hard link file:

```
[root@localhost ~]$ ls -l myhosts
-rw-r--r-- 2 root root 186 Jul 11  2015 myhosts
```

To view the inode number of a file, use the **-i** option to the **ls** command:

```
ls -i myhosts
263402 myhosts
```

Then use the **find** command to search for files with the same inode:

```
[root@localhost ~]$ find / -inum 263402 -ls 2> /dev/null
263402    4 -rw-r--r--  2 root    root      186 Jul 11  2015 /root/
myhosts
263402    4 -rw-r--r--  2 root    root      186 Jul 11  2015 /etc/hosts
```

## CHAPTER 23

Find System Files and Place Files in the Correct Location

This chapter provides information and commands concerning the following topics:

- Understand the correct locations of files under the FHS
- Find files and commands on a Linux system
- Know the location and purpose of important files and directories as defined in the FHS
- **find**
- **locate**
- **updatedb**
- **whereis**
- **which**
- **type**
- **/etc/updatedb.conf**

Understand the Correct Locations of Files Under the FHS

The Filesystem Hierarchy Standard (FHS) is a definition of where files and directories are supposed to be placed on Unix and Linux operating systems. A summary of some of the more important locations is provided in the following table:

Location	Description/contents
/	The root or top-level directory.
/bin	Critical binary executables.
/boot	Files related to booting the system.
/etc	Configuration files for the system.
/home	Regular user home directories.
/lib	Critical system libraries.
/media	Location of mount points for removable media.
/mnt	Location for temporary mounts.
/opt	Optional software packages.
/proc	Information related to kernel data and process data. (This is a virtual filesystem, not a disk-based filesystem.)
/root	Home directory for the root user account.
/sbin	Critical system binary executables.
/tmp	Location for temporary files.

Location	Description/contents
/usr	Location for many subdirectories that contain binary executables, libraries, and documentation.
/usr/bin	Nonessential binary executables.
/usr/lib	Libraries for the executables in the **/usr/bin** directory.
/usr/sbin	Nonessential system binary executables.
/usr/share	Data that is architecture-independent.
/var	Data that is variable (changes in size regularly).
/var/mail	Mail logs.
/var/log	Spool data (such as print spools).
/var/tmp	Temporary files.

Find Files and Commands on a Linux System

See the "find" and "locate" sections in this chapter for details.

Know the Location and Purpose of Important Files and Directories as Defined in the FHS

See the "Understand the Correct Locations of Files Under the FHS" section in this chapter for details.

find

Use the **find** command to search the live filesystem for files based on name or other file metadata.

Syntax:

```
find starting_directory criteria outcome
```

Notes based on this syntax:

- Consider the *starting_directory* carefully. Starting the search from / can take a long time.
- The *criteria* would be a combination of an option and an argument (for example, **-name "test"**).
- The *outcome* is what the **find** command will do with the output. The default action, if no *outcome* option is provided, is to simply print the filename that was found.

For search criteria that require numeric arguments, the following values may be used:

- +n—More than *n*
- -n—Less than *n*
- n—Exactly equal to *n*

Important criteria options include the following:

Option	Description
-amin *n*	Search by access timestamp in *n* minutes. For example, to find all files accessed within the last 20 minutes, use **-amin -20**.
-atime *n*	Search by access timestamp in days (actually, *n*+24 hours).
-cmin *n*	Search by status change timestamp in *n* minutes; *status change* is when metadata, such as ownership or permissions, has last changed.
-ctime *n*	Search by status change timestamp in days (actually, *n*+24 hours); *status change* is when metadata, such as ownership or permissions, has last changed.
-group *name*	Search by group ownership (group *name*); use **-gid** to match by GID (group ID).
-iname *pattern*	Perform a case-insensitive search for files that have names that match *pattern*; the pattern can include glob characters of *, ?, and [ ].
-iregex *pattern*	Perform a case-insensitive search for files that have names that match the specified regular expression's *pattern*.
-mmin *n*	Search by modification timestamp in *n* minutes; *modification* means the file contents have changed.
-mtime *n*	Search by modification timestamp in days (actually, *n*+24 hours); *modification* means the file contents have changed.
-name *pattern*	Perform a case-sensitive search for files that have names that match *pattern*; the pattern can include glob characters of *, ?, and [ ].
-perm *mode*	Search for files with permissions exactly as specified by *mode*; the mode can be octal (**0755**) or symbolic (**u=rw**). Because all permissions must match exactly, using **u=rw** will only match files with the permissions of **rw-------**.
-perm *-mode*	Search for files with permissions that are set as specified by *mode*; the mode can be symbolic (**u=rw**) only. Because only the permissions specified are matched, using **u=rw** will match files with the permissions of **rw** for the owner, regardless of any other permissions.
-regex *pattern*	Perform a case-sensitive search for files that have names that match the specified regular expression's *pattern*.
-size *n*	Match file based on file size. Sizes can be given in bytes (b), kilobytes (k), megabytes (M), and gigabytes (G). Example: **-size +100M**.
-type *value*	Match file based on file type. Types can be specified as block (**b**), character (**c**), directory (**d**), regular file (**f**), and symbolic link (**l**).
-user *name*	Search by user ownership (user *name*); use **-uid** to match by UID (user ID) .

Important outcome options include the following:

Option	Description
-delete	Attempt to delete files that are found.
-exec *cmd* {} \;	Execute the command specified by *cmd* on the file.
-ls	Provide details about files found, much like the **ls -l** command.
-ok *cmd* {} \;	Execute the command specified by *cmd* on the file, but only after prompting the user to determine if the command should be executed.
-print	Display the filename only for each matched file. (This is the default outcome action.)

locate

The **locate** command searches for files based on a database that is typically created daily. It does not search the live filesystem, which means it can't be used to find recent files. However, the **location** command performs its searches quicker than the **find** command because searching a database is faster than searching the live filesystem.

Example:

```
[student@localhost ~]$ locate passwd.1.gz
/usr/share/man/cs/man1/gpasswd.1.gz
/usr/share/man/de/man1/gpasswd.1.gz
/usr/share/man/fr/man1/gpasswd.1.gz
/usr/share/man/hu/man1/gpasswd.1.gz
/usr/share/man/it/man1/gpasswd.1.gz
/usr/share/man/ja/man1/gpasswd.1.gz
/usr/share/man/ja/man1/passwd.1.gz
/usr/share/man/man1/gpasswd.1.gz
/usr/share/man/man1/htpasswd.1.gz
/usr/share/man/man1/kpasswd.1.gz
/usr/share/man/man1/ldappasswd.1.gz
/usr/share/man/man1/lpasswd.1.gz
/usr/share/man/man1/lppasswd.1.gz
/usr/share/man/man1/passwd.1.gz
/usr/share/man/pt_BR/man1/gpasswd.1.gz
/usr/share/man/ru/man1/gpasswd.1.gz
/usr/share/man/zh_CN/man1/gpasswd.1.gz
```

Important options include the following:

Option	Description
-i	Perform a case-insensitive search.
-r	Use regular expressions rather than globbing when matching file-names.

See the "updatedb" and "/etc/updatedb.conf" sections in this chapter for more details regarding the database used by the **locate** command.

updatedb

The database used by the **locate** command is created by the **updatedb** command. This command is typically executed automatically by a cron job, on a daily basis, but can also be executed manually by the root user.

See the "/etc/updatedb.conf" section in this chapter for more details regarding the database used by the **locate** command.

whereis

The **whereis** command searches for binary executables, source code, and manual pages. It makes use of standard locations as well as variables such as **$PATH** and **$MANPATH** to determine where to search.

Example:

```
[student@localhost ~]$ whereis ls
ls: /usr/bin/ls /usr/share/man/man1/ls.1.gz /usr/share/man/man1p/
ls.1p.gz
```

Important options include the following:

Option	Description
-b	Search only for matching executable binary files.
-m	Search only for matching man pages.
-s	Search only for matching source code files.

which

The **whereis** command searches for binary executables. It will report back if the command specified is an alias and will search the locations of the **$PATH** variable. Here are some examples:

```
[student@localhost ~]$ echo $PATH
/usr/local/bin:/bin:/usr/bin:/usr/local/sbin:/usr/sbin:/home/student/.
local/bin:/home/student/bin
[student@localhost ~]$ which ls
alias ls='ls --color=auto'
        /bin/ls
[student@localhost ~]$ which awk
/bin/awk
[student@localhost ~]$ which rougeone
/usr/bin/which: no rougeone in (/usr/local/bin:/bin:/usr/bin:
/usr/local/sbin:/usr/sbin:/home/student/.local/bin:/home/student/bin)
```

Important options include the following:

Option	Description
-a	Display all matches; the **which** command normally exits after the first match is made.
--skip-alias	Do not search for the alias.
-s	Search only for the matching source code files.

See the "type" section in this chapter for details regarding a similar command.

type

Similar to the **which** command, the **type** command will search for executable commands. However, the **type** command also searches for internal (built-in) bash shell commands. Here are some examples:

```
[student@localhost ~]$ type ls
ls is aliased to `ls --color=auto'
[student@localhost ~]$ type awk
awk is /bin/awk
[student@localhost ~]$ type cd
cd is a shell builtin
[student@localhost ~]$ which cd
/bin/cd
```

> **NOTE:** When you execute a command, the following is the order in which the shell searches for the command:
>
> 1. Built-in shell commands
> 2. Aliases
> 3. Commands found in the directories in the **$PATH** variable (in the order they are listed in the variable)

See the "which" section in this chapter for details regarding a similar command.

/etc/updatedb.conf

When the **updatedb** command is executed, it creates a database of all files on the operating system. The database is created based on rules stored in the **/etc/updatedb.conf** file. A typical file will look like the following:

```
[student@localhost ~]$ more /etc/updatedb.conf
PRUNE_BIND_MOUNTS = "yes"
PRUNEFS = "9p afs anon_inodefs auto autofs bdev binfmt_misc cgroup cifs
coda configfs cpuset debugfs de
vpts ecryptfs exofs fuse fuse.sshfs fusectl gfs gfs2 hugetlbfs inoti-
fyfs iso9660 jffs2 lustre mqueue nc
pfs nfs nfs4 nfsd pipefs proc ramfs rootfs rpc_pipefs securityfs
selinuxfs sfs sockfs sysfs tmpfs ubifs
 udf usbfs"
```

```
PRUNENAMES = ".git .hg .svn"
PRUNEPATHS = "/afs /media /mnt /net /sfs /tmp /udev /var/cache/ccache /
var/lib/yum/yumdb /var/spool/cup
s /var/spool/squid /var/tmp"
```

Important settings in the **/etc/updatedb.conf** file include the following:

Setting	Description
PRUNEFS	Indicates that files on the specified filesystems will not be included in the database.
PRUNENAMES	Indicates that files that match the specified patterns will not be included in the database.
PRUNEPATHS	Indicates that files in the specified directories will not be included in the database.

See the "updatedb" and "locate" sections in this chapter for more details.

## CHAPTER 24

Customize and Use the Shell Environment

This chapter provides information and commands concerning the following topics:

- Set environment variables (for example, PATH) at login or when spawning a new shell
- Write bash functions for frequently used sequences of commands
- Maintain skeleton directories for new user accounts
- Set command search path with the proper directory
- **source**
- **/etc/bash.bashrc**
- **/etc/profile**
- **env**
- **export**
- **set**
- **unset**
- **~/.bash_profile**
- **~/.bash_login**
- **~/.profile**
- **~/.bashrc**
- **~/.bash_logout**
- Function
- Alias
- Lists

Set Environment Variables (For Example, PATH) at Login or When Spawning a New Shell

When a user logs in to the system, a login shell is started. When a user starts a new shell after login, it is referred to as a *non-login shell*. In each case, initialization files are used to set up the shell environment. Which initialization files are executed depends on whether the shell is a login shell or a non-login shell.

Figure 24.1 demonstrates which initialization files are executed when the user logs in to the system.

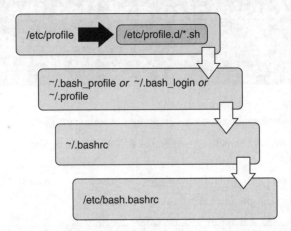

Figure 24.1 Initialization Files Executed When the User Logs In to the System

The following is an explanation of Figure 24.1:

- The first initialization file that is executed when a user logs in is the **/etc/profile** file. On most Linux platforms, this script includes code that executes all the initialization files in the **/etc/profile.d** directory that end in ".sh". *The purpose of the /etc/profile file is to be a place for system administrators to put code that will execute every time every bash shell user logs in (typically login messages and environment variable definitions).*

- After the **/etc/profile** file is executed, the login shell looks in the user's home directory for a file named **~/.bash_profile**. If it's found, the login shell executes the code in this file. Otherwise, the login shell looks for a file named **~/.bash_login**. If it's found, the login shell executes the code in this file. Otherwise, then the login shell looks for a file named **~/.profile** and executes the code in this file. *The purpose of these files is to be a place where each user can put code that will execute every time that specific user logs in (typically environment variable definitions).*

- The next initialization file executed is the **~/.bashrc** script. *The purpose of this file is to be a place where each user can put code that will execute every time the user opens a new shell (typically alias and function definitions).*

- The next initialization file executed is the **/etc/bash.bashrc** script. *The purpose of this file is to be a place where system administrators can put code that will execute every time the user opens a new shell (typically alias and function definitions).*

Figure 24.2 demonstrates which initialization files are executed when the user opens a new shell.

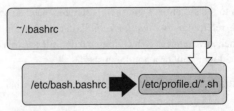

Figure 24.2 Initialization Files Executed When the User Starts a Non-Login Shell

The following is an explanation of Figure 24.2:

- The first initialization file that is executed when a user opens a non-login shell is the ~/.bashrc script. *The purpose of this file is to be a place where each user can put code that will execute every time that user opens a new shell (typically alias and function definitions).*

- The next initialization file executed is the /etc/bash.bashrc script. On most Linux platforms, this script includes code that executes all the initialization files in the /etc/profile.d directory that end in ".sh". *The purpose of these initialization files is to be a place where system administrators can put code that will execute every time the user opens a new shell (typically alias and function definitions).*

Write Bash Functions for Frequently Used Sequences of Commands

See the "functions" section in this chapter for details.

Maintain Skeleton Directories for New User Accounts

When a new user account is created, default configuration files can be automatically placed with the new user's home directory via skeleton directories. These skeleton directories contain copies of the configuration files. When using the **useradd** command, you can use the **-k** option to specify the location of the skeleton directory:

```
useradd -k /etc/skel julia
```

The default skeleton directory is /etc/skel. Different directories can be created for different types of users.

Set Command Search Path with the Proper Directory

When a user executes a command, the bash shell looks for this command in specific locations. The locations it searches are displayed here in the order in which the search is conducted:

1. Built-in shell commands

2. Aliases and functions

3. Locations specified in the $PATH variable

For example, there is both a built-in **echo** command and an **echo** command in the /bin directory (which is included in a typical $PATH variable). If a user executes the **echo** command, then the built-in **echo** command is executed. To execute the other **echo** command, the user would have to type the complete path to the command: /bin/echo.

source

Most commands are executed as separate processes that have their own environment. The **source** command allows you to execute a bash script as if the commands within the script were executed directly on the command line.

Example:

```
[root@localhost ~]$ source ./functions.sh
```

Use the **.** command to perform the same function as the **source** command:

```
[root@localhost ~]$ . ./functions.sh
```

/etc/bash.bashrc

When a user opens a new bash shell, the commands in the **/etc/bash.bashrc** file are executed. Only the root user should be allowed to modify the **/etc/bash.bashrc** file. This provides the root user with the ability to set up all bash user accounts by placing commands in this file.

See the "Set Environment Variables (For Example, PATH) at Login or When Spawning a New Shell" section in this chapter for additional details.

/etc/profile

When a user logs in to the system and the user's login shell is a bash shell, the commands in the **/etc/profile** file are executed. Only the root user should be allowed to modify the **/etc/profile** file. This allows the root user the ability to set up all bash user accounts by placing commands in this file.

See the "Set Environment Variables (For Example, PATH) at Login or When Spawning a New Shell" section in this chapter for additional details.

env

Use the **env** command to run a command in an alternative environment. For example, the following commands execute the **date** command in the native environment and an environment with a different time zone setting via the use of the **TZ** variable:

```
[student @localhost ~]$ date
Wed Jan 25 13:39:09 UTC 2017
[student@localhost ~]$ env TZ=PDT date
Wed Jan 25 13:40:23 PDT 2017
```

Important options for the **env** command include the following:

Option	Description
-i	Do not inherit the environment from the parent shell, but rather begin with an empty environment.
-u	Unset an environment variable (for example, **env -u VAR**).

export

The **export** command converts a local variable into an environment variable:

```
[student @localhost ~]$ TODAY="March 19"
[student @localhost ~]$ export TODAY
```

A new variable can be made an environment variable by using the **export** command:

```
[student @localhost ~]$ export TOMORROW="March 20"
```

When the **export** command is executed with no arguments, it will display all the environment variables in the current shell.

set

The **set** command displays all the variables and functions in the current shell.

unset

The **unset** command is used to remove a variable from the current shell:

```
[student @localhost ~]$ dir="/etc"
[student @localhost ~]$ echo $dir
/etc
[student @localhost ~]$ unset dir
[student @localhost ~]$ echo $dir

[student @localhost ~]$
```

~/.bash_profile

When a user logs in to the system and the user's login shell is a bash shell, the commands in the **~/.bash_profile** file are executed if this file exists. This provides the user with the ability to set up their account by placing commands in this file.

See the "Set Environment Variables (For Example, PATH) at Login or When Spawning a New Shell" section in this chapter for additional details.

~/.bash_login

When a user logs in to the system and the user's login shell is a bash shell, the commands in the ~/.bash_login file are executed if this file exists. This allows the user the ability to set up their account by placing commands in this file.

See the "Set Environment Variables (For Example, PATH) at Login or When Spawning a New Shell" section in this chapter for additional details.

~/.profile

When a user logs in to the system and the user's login shell is a bash shell, the commands in the ~/.profile file are executed if this file exists. This allows the user the ability to set up their account by placing commands in this file.

See the "Set Environment Variables (For Example, PATH) at Login or When Spawning a New Shell" section in this chapter for additional details.

~/.bashrc

When a user opens a new bash shell, the commands in the ~/.bashrc file are executed. This allows the user the ability to set up their account by placing commands in this file.

See the "Set Environment Variables (For Example, PATH) at Login or When Spawning a New Shell" section in this chapter for additional details.

~/.bash_logout

When a user logs off, all the commands in the ~/.bash_logout file are executed.

Function

Similar to an alias, a *function* is a feature that allows a collection of commands to be executed by issuing a single "command." Here's how to create a function:

```
[student @localhost ~]$ list () {
> ls -ld $1
> }
```

The $1 in the previous example refers to the first argument of the **list()** function. For example, the function could now be called in the following manner:

```
[student @localhost ~]$ list /etc
drwxr-xr-x 97 root root 4096 Jan 23 08:40 /etc
```

Each shell has its own functions that can be displayed by executing the **set** command. To create persistent functions (functions that are re-created for each new shell), place the function definition in the ~/.bashrc file.

Alias

Similar to a function, an *alias* is a feature that allows a collection of commands to be
executed by issuing a single "command." Here's how to create an alias:

```
[student @localhost ~]$ alias copy="cp"
```

And here's how to use an alias:

```
[student @localhost ~]$ ls
file.txt
[student @localhost ~]$ copy /etc/hosts .
[student @localhost ~]$ ls
file.txt  hosts
```

To display all aliases, execute the **alias** command with no arguments. To unset an alias,
use the **unalias** command:

```
[student @localhost ~]$ alias
alias copy='cp'
alias egrep='egrep --color=auto'
alias fgrep='fgrep --color=auto'
alias grep='grep --color=auto'
alias l='ls -CF'
alias la='ls -A'
alias ll='ls -alF'
[student @localhost ~]$ unalias copy
[student @localhost ~]$ alias
alias egrep='egrep --color=auto'
alias fgrep='fgrep --color=auto'
alias grep='grep --color=auto'
alias l='ls -CF'
alias la='ls -A'
alias ll='ls -alF'
```

Lists

A bash shell list is a variable that contains a collection of commands. The two primary
list methods are called *logical or* and *logical and*:

- cmd1 || cmd2
- cmd1 && cmd2

Each command returns a success or failure value to the shell. If you execute the com-
mand list **cmd1 || cmd2**, then the second command is only executed if the first command
returns a failure value. If you execute the command list **cmd1 && cmd2**, then the second command is only executed if the first command returns a success value.

## CHAPTER 25

Customize or Write Simple Scripts

This chapter provides information and commands concerning the following topics:

- Use standard sh syntax (loops, tests)
- Use command substitution
- Test return values for success or failure or other information provided by a command
- Perform conditional mailing to the superuser
- Correctly select the script interpreter through the shebang (#!) line
- Manage the location, ownership, execution, and suid-rights of scripts
- **for**
- **while**
- **test**
- **if**
- **read**
- **seq**
- **exec**

Use Standard sh Syntax (Loops, Tests)

See the "for," "while," "test," and "if" sections in this chapter.

Use Command Substitution

Command substitution is the process of executing a sub-command within a larger command. This is typically used to gather data and store it into a variable. For example, the following command stores the output of the **date** command into the **$today** variable:

```
today=$(date)
```

Command substitution can be performed by using one of two methods:

- **$(cmd)**
- **`cmd`**

Note that the second method uses backquote characters (also called *backtick* characters), not single-quote characters.

Test Return Values for Success or Failure or Other Information Provided by a Command

When a command executes, it returns a value of success (0) or failure (>1) to the shell or script from which it was executed. This status is stored in the **$?** variable. Here's an example:

```
[root@localhost ~]$ ls /etc/skel
[root@localhost ~]$ echo $?
0
[root@localhost ~]$ ls /junk
ls: cannot access /junk: No such file or directory
[root@localhost ~]$ echo $?
2
```

This return value can be used in conditional statements to determine if a command exited successfully:

```
some_command
if [ $? -eq 0 ]
then
    echo "command executed successfully"
else
    echo "command failed"
fi
```

See the "test" and "if" sections in this chapter for additional details.

Perform Conditional Mailing to the Superuser

To send a message via mail to the superuser (root user) in the event that a command fails, use the following syntax:

```
some_command || mail -s "subject line" root
```

Correctly Select the Script Interpreter through the Shebang (#!) Line

The first line of a script should include the path to the interpreter. For bash shell scripts, this should be the path to the executable **bash** command. This path can be discovered by executing the following command:

```
[root@localhost ~]$ which bash
/bin/bash
```

Add this path to the first line of the script using the following syntax:

```
#!/bin/bash
```

The combination of the # character (the hash character) and the ! character (the bang character) forms the shebang sequence. (Say "hash bang" quickly to discover where the term *shebang* comes from; often it will be said with a silent *e*).

Manage the Location, Ownership, Execution and suid-rights of scripts

Scripts should be located in one of the directories defined by the **$PATH** variable:

```
[root@localhost ~]$ echo $PATH
/usr/local/sbin:/usr/local/bin:/usr/sbin:/usr/bin:/sbin:/bin:
/usr/games:/usr/local/games
```

Often only the root user will be able to place a file in one of these directories, so regular users can make their own directory and add it to the **$PATH** variable:

```
[root@localhost ~]$ mkdir /home/bob/bin
[root@localhost ~]$ PATH="$PATH:/home/bob/bin"
```

Scripts should be owned by regular users, not the root user. Running scripts owned by root can result in security issues. If a script is owned by root, it should never have the suid permission set on it because this results in a serious security risk (most modern Linux distributions don't permit suid, root-owned scripts).

After creating a script, add execute permission to run it like a program:

```
chmod a+x script_name
```

for

A **for** loop is used to iterate over a list of values. For example, the following will execute the **wc -l** command on a list of files:

```
for file in "/etc/r*.conf"
do
    wc -l $file
done
```

Sample output:

```
43 /etc/request-key.conf
 3 /etc/resolv.conf
61 /etc/rsyslog.conf
```

while

A **while** loop is designed to perform a set of tasks (commands) as long as a conditional statement returns a value of true. For example, the following code can be used to check user input to verify the correct value is provided:

```
read -p "Enter a zip code: "
while echo $zip | egrep -v "^[0-9]{5}$"
do
    echo "$zip is not a valid ZIP code, try again"
    read -p "Enter a zip code" zip
done
```

Sample output:

```
Enter a zip code: 8888
8888 is not a valid ZIP code, try again
Enter a zip code: huh?
huh? is not a valid ZIP code, try again
Enter a zip code: 92020
```

See the "read" section in this chapter for information about the **read** command.

test

The **test** statement is used to perform conditional tests. These conditional tests are used to compare values and perform file-testing operations.

A common method of running the **test** statement is to place the operation within square brackets. For example, the following two statements perform the same action:

```
test $name1 = $name2
[ $name1 = $name2 ]
```

The following table describes the common **test** operations:

Operation	Description
str1 = str2	Returns true if two strings are equal to each other.
str1 != str2	Returns true if two strings are not equal to each other.
-z str	Returns true if *str* size is zero; for example, [-z $name].
-n str	Returns true if *str* size is not zero; for example, [-n $name].
int1 -eq int2	Returns true if two integers are equal to each other.
int1 -ne int2	Returns true if two integers are not equal to each other.
int1 -gt int2	Returns true if the first integer is greater than the second integer.
int1 -ge int2	Returns true if the first integer is greater than or equal to the second integer.
int1 -lt int2	Returns true if the first integer is less than the second integer.
int1 -le int2	Returns true if the first integer is less than or equal to the second integer.
-d file	Returns true if the file is a directory.

Operation	Description
-f file	Returns true if the file is a plain file.
-e file	Returns true if the file exists (regardless of what type of file or directory it is).
-r file	Returns true if the file is readable.
-w file	Returns true if the file is writable.
-x file	Returns true if the file is executable.

if

An **if** statement is used to execute one or more commands based on the outcome of a conditional statement. For example, the following will display "hi" if the **$name** variable is set to "Bob":

```
if [ $name = "Bob" ]
then
    echo "hi"
fi
```

Note that to end the commands executed within an **if** statement, use the **fi** statement ("if" spelled backwards).

An **else** statement is used with an **if** statement to provide an alternative in the event that the condition returns false. Here's an example:

```
if [ $name = "Bob" ]
then
    echo "hi"
else
    echo "I don't know you"
fi
```

Multiple conditional checks can be performed, like so:

```
if [ $name = "Bob" ]
then
    echo "hi, Bob"
elif [ $name = "Sue" ]
then
    echo "hi, Sue"
else
    echo "I don't know you"
fi
```

See the "test" section in this chapter for additional information on conditional expressions.

read

The **read** statement will extract information from STDIN (standard input) and place the extracted data into one or more variables. For example, the following will read data from STDIN and place the data into the **$name** variable:

```
read name
```

To assign values to different variables, use the following syntax:

```
read var1 var2 var3
```

Use the **-p** option to issue a prompt to the user:

```
read -p "Enter your name" name
```

seq

The **seq** command returns a sequence of numeric values:

```
[root@localhost ~]$ seq 1 10
1
2
3
4
5
6
7
8
9
10
```

Use the **-s** option to change the separator:

```
[root@localhost ~]$ seq -s ":" 1 10
1:2:3:4:5:6:7:8:9:10
[root@localhost ~]$ seq -s " " 1 10
1 2 3 4 5 6 7 8 9 10
```

exec

Use the **exec** command to launch a process that replaces the current bash shell. This is typically used at the end of a script to replace the script with another process. Here's an example:

```
exec /usr/bin/custom_cmd
```

## CHAPTER 26

SQL Data Management

This chapter provides information and commands concerning the following topics:

- Use of basic SQL commands
- Perform basic data manipulation
- **insert**
- **update**
- **select**
- **delete**
- **from**
- **where**
- **group by**
- **order by**
- **join**

Use of Basic SQL Commands

See the "insert," "update," "select," and "delete" sections in this chapter.

Perform Basic Data Manipulation

See the "group by," "order by," and "join" sections in this chapter.

insert

The **insert** command is used to add (insert) a record or records into a SQL table. The syntax of this command is as follows:

```
INSERT INTO table
VALUES (value, value, value,....)
```

or

```
INSERT INTO table
(column, column, column,...)
VALUES (value, value, value,....)
```

Example:

```
INSERT INTO Birthdays (Name, Day)
VALUES ('Nick', 'April 20');
```

update

The **update** command is used to update a field or multiple **fields** in a record or multiple records. The syntax of this command is as follows:

```
UPDATE table
SET column1=value1,column2=value2,...
WHERE some_column=some_value;
```

Example:

```
UPDATE Birthdays
SET Day='April 21'
WHERE Name='Nick'
```

select

The **select** command is used to pull information from a table and return a result. The syntax of this command is as follows:

```
SELECT column1,column2,...
FROM table;
```

This first example returns only the Day column from the Birthday table:

```
SELECT Day
FROM Birthdays
```

This next example returns all columns from the Birthday table:

```
SELECT * FROM Birthdays;
```

delete

The **update** command is used to delete records in a SQL table. The syntax of this command is as follows:

```
DELETE FROM table
WHERE some_column=some_value;
```

Example:

```
DELETE FROM Birthdays
WHERE Name='Nick'
```

from

The **from** command is used to indicate which table to perform another command on. See the "select" and "delete" sections in this chapter for more details.

where

The **where** command is used to indicate specific criteria to run a command on, such as if a specific value occurs in a column. See the "update" and "delete" sections in this chapter for more details.

group by

The **group by** function is often used when aggregate functions are called in order to group results by column. The syntax of this function is as follows:

```
SELECT column, function(column)
FROM table
WHERE column operator value
GROUP BY column;
```

order by

The **order by** clause sorts the data based on a single column or multiple columns. The order can be in either ascending or descending order. The syntax of this clause is as follows:

```
SELECT column
FROM table
[WHERE condition]
[ORDER BY column1, column2, .. columnN] [ASC | DESC];
```

join

The **join** statement is used to merge columns from two separate tables. The **join** statement is used to merge together columns from two separate tables into a new table. The **join** statement is a clause of the **from** statement.

The syntax of this statement is as follows:

```
SELECT column
FROM table1 JOIN table2
ON column1 = column2
WHERE condition
```

## CHAPTER 27

Install and Configure X11

This chapter provides information and commands concerning the following topics:

- Verify that the video card and monitor are supported by an X server
- Awareness of the X font server
- Basic understanding and knowledge of the X Window configuration file
- **/etc/X11/xorg.conf**
- **xhost**
- **DISPLAY**
- **xwininfo**
- **xdpyinfo**
- **X**

Verify That the Video Card and Monitor Are Supported by an X Server

See the "X" section in this chapter.

Awareness of the X Font Server

The X font server (xfs) provides fonts to the X Window server. To use this server, add the following to the **/etc/X11/xorg.conf** file:

```
FontPath "unix/:7100"
```

Basic Understanding and Knowledge of the X Window Configuration File

See the "/etc/X11/xorg.conf" section in this chapter.

/etc/X11/xorg.conf

The **/etc/X11/xorg.conf** file is the primary configuration file for the X server. The file is broken into different configuration sections, including the following:

Section	Description
Files	Used to specify pathnames to files needed by the server; for example, the **FontPath** entry is used to indicate the location for fonts.
ServerFlags	Provides global X server options.

Section	Description
Module	Loads X server modules; for example, to load the DRI module, include **Load "dri"** in the **Module** section.
Extensions	Enables X11 protocol extensions.
InputDevice	Used to define input devices such as mouse and keyboard.
Device	Used to define output devices such as video cards.
Monitor	Defines the monitor or monitors connected to the system.
Screen	Matches the device (video card) to the corresponding attached monitor.

Here's a sample **/etc/X11/xorg.conf** file:

```
Section "Module"
    Load        "dbe"
    Load        "ddc"
EndSection
Section "Extensions"
    Option  "Composite"     "Enable"
EndSection
Section "Files"
    FontPath    "/usr/X11/lib/X11/fonts/75dpi/:unscaled"
    FontPath    "/usr/X11/lib/X11/fonts/100dpi/:unscaled"
    FontPath    "/usr/X11/lib/X11/fonts/misc/"
EndSection
Section "InputDevice"
    Identifier  "Keyboard1"
    Driver      "kbd"
EndSection
Section "InputDevice"
    Identifier  "Mouse1"
    Driver      "mouse"
    Option "Protocol"      "Microsoft"
    Option "Device"        "/dev/input/mice"
EndSection
Section "Monitor"
    Identifier  "Monitor1"
EndSection
Section "Device"
    Identifier    "Card1"
    Driver        "fbdev"
    Option        "fbdev" "/dev/fb0"
EndSection
Section "Screen"
    Identifier    "Screen1"
    Device        "Card1"
```

```
Monitor      "Monitor1"
DefaultDepth 24
Subsection "Display"
     Modes       "1024x768" "800x600" "640x480"
EndSubsection
EndSection
Section "ServerLayout"
   Identifier   "Simple Layout"
   Screen "Screen1"
   InputDevice "Mouse1" "CorePointer"
   InputDevice "Keyboard1" "CoreKeyboard"
EndSection
```

> **NOTE:**   Although **xorg.conf** is typically located in the **/etc/X11** directory, its location may vary across operating system distributions. (See manual page "man xorg.conf" for details and further possible locations.)

xhost

The **xhost** command is used to provide access to an X Window server. Typically only the user who logged in to the X Window server can display GUI-based applications on that server. To allow all users this access, use the following command:

xhost +

To turn off this access, use this command:

xhost -

Access can be granted to users from a specific host, like so, but you cannot indicate which users from that host can have access (all users are granted access):

xhost +server25

Access is removed for a specific host via the following command:

xhost -server25

With no arguments, the **xhost** command displays the current access rules.

DISPLAY

The DISPLAY variable is used to determine where to send graphic output. Typically it is either unset, which defaults to the local display, or set to **":0.0"** (also the local display):

```
[student@localhost ~]$ echo $DISPLAY


[student@localhost ~]$ export DISPLAY=":0.0"
[student@localhost ~]$ echo $DISPLAY
:0.0
```

After logging in to a remote system, you might need to set the display to your local system in order to execute GUI-based commands and have the output be displayed on the local system.

xwininfo

The **xwininfo** command is used to display information about a specific window (GUI-base application). Important options for the **xwininfo** command include the following:

Option	Description
-all	Used to display all window information.
-children	Displays the root, parent, and child windows' information.
-tree	Like the **-children** option, but will display all child windows recursively.
-stats	Provides additional statistical output.

Sample output:

```
[student@localhost ~]$ xwininfo -tree -all

xwininfo: Please select the window about which you
          would like information by clicking the
          mouse in that window.

xwininfo: Window id: 0x2600e26 "student@server:~/Desktop"

  Root window id: 0x17b (the root window) (has no name)
  Parent window id: 0x180028f (has no name)
     1 child:
     0x2600e27 (has no name): ()  1x1+-1+-1  +0+66

  Absolute upper-left X:  1
  Absolute upper-left Y:  67
  Relative upper-left X:  10
  Relative upper-left Y:  47
  Width: 735
  Height: 463
  Depth: 32
  Visual: 0x4f
  Visual Class: TrueColor
  Border width: 0
  Class: InputOutput
  Colormap: 0x2600006 (not installed)
  Bit Gravity State: NorthWestGravity
  Window Gravity State: NorthWestGravity
```

Backing Store State: NotUseful

Save Under State: no

Map State: IsViewable

Override Redirect State: no

Corners: +1+67   -864+67   -864-183   +1-183

-geometry 80x24+-9+20

Bit gravity: NorthWestGravity

Window gravity: NorthWestGravity

Backing-store hint: NotUseful

Backing-planes to be preserved: 0xffffffff

Backing pixel: 0

Save-unders: No

Someone wants these events:

    Exposure

    VisibilityChange

    StructureNotify

    PropertyChange

Do not propagate these events:

Override redirection?: No

Window manager hints:

    Client accepts input or input focus: Yes

    Initial state is Normal State

    Displayed on desktop 0

    Window type:

        Normal

    Process id: 4784 on host server.sample999.com

    Frame extents: 1, 1, 39, 1

Normal window size hints:

    Program supplied minimum size: 306 by 71

    Program supplied base size: 15 by 31

    Program supplied x resize increment: 9

    Program supplied y resize increment: 18

    Program supplied minimum size in resize increments: 34 by 3

    Program supplied base size in resize increments: 1 by 1

    Program supplied window gravity: NorthWestGravity

No zoom window size hints defined

No window shape defined

No border shape defined

xdpyinfo

The **xdpyinfo** command is used to display information about the currently running X server. The output for this command can exceed 1000 lines, so a brief summary is displayed in the following example:

```
[student@localhost ~]$ xdpyinfo | head
name of display:    :0.0
version number:    11.0
vendor string:    The X.Org Foundation
vendor release number:    11702000
X.Org version: 1.17.2
maximum request size:  16777212 bytes
motion buffer size:  256
bitmap unit, bit order, padding:    32, LSBFirst, 32
image byte order:    LSBFirst
number of supported pixmap formats:    7
```

The **xdpyinfo** command has only a handful of options, none of which are typically used.

X

The **X** command starts the X server, but not any additional programs, such as a desktop or login screen (called a display manager). This command is useful when you're troubleshooting your X server, but is rarely used for any other purpose.

One of the primary uses of the **X** command is to ensure that the X server supports the video card and monitor attached to the system. Because X only starts the X server, if this command fails, then one possible cause could be an unsupported video card or monitor.

## CHAPTER 28

Set Up a Display Manager

This chapter provides information and commands concerning the following topics:

- Basic configuration of LightDM
- Turn the display manager on or off
- Change the display manager greeting
- Awareness of XDM, KDM, and GDM
- lightdm
- **/etc/lightdm**

Basic Configuration of LightDM

See the "/etc/lightdm" section in this chapter.

Turn the Display Manager On or Off

To be clear, you don't turn on or off a display manager. You can change from one display manager to another, and you can turn off the X Window server, but if you have the X Window server starting as boot, you really must have a display manager available.

On Debian-based systems, including Ubuntu and Mint, to change the display manager, run the **dpkg-reconfigure gdm** command or modify the **/etc/X11/default-display** manager file. This file should only have the path to the display manager.

On Red Hat–based systems, including CentOS and Fedora, an older method to change the display manager is to modify the **/etc/sysconfig/desktop** file and include the following setting:

```
DISPLAYMANAGER="KDE" #or GDM, XDM, etc.
```

The newer method on Red Hat–based systems is to use the following command:

```
systemctl enable lightdm.service
```

In all these cases, changing the display manger requires root access.

Change the Display Manager Greeting

The display manager greeting is the message that is displayed to the user when the user is presented with a login screen. The exact technique to change a display manager greeting depends on the display manager itself. Most display managers have a configuration section called either "greet," "greeting," or "greeter." Within that configuration section, there will be a setting called **GreetMessage** or something similar. Find this setting and modify the value to change the display manager greeting.

Awareness of XDM, KDM, and GDM

XDM, KDM, and GDM are display managers—programs that allow you to log in to a GUI environment. These programs also start the desktop for the user as the user logs in.

The following table provides the basic information for these display managers:

Option	Configuration File(s) Location	Description
XDM	/etc/X11/xdm directory	Basic display manager provided with the X server software. Rarely used because it doesn't have the features that are provided by KDM and GDM. Executable: **/usr/bin/xdm**.
KDM	/etc/kde/kdm directory	Default display manager of the KDE software suite. Normally used when KDE is installed, but it can start other desktops besides the KDE desktop. Executable: **/usr/bin/kdm**.
GDM	/etc/gdm directory	Default display manager of the Gnome software suite. Normally used when Gnome is installed, but it can start other desktops besides the Gnome desktop. Executable: **/usr/sbin/gdm**.

lightdm

One of the newer display managers is lightdm, which is often the default display manager for "cutting-edge" distributions such as Ubuntu. There are literally dozens of display managers, but lately lightdm has become one of the more popular ones.

To configure lightdm, modify the contents of the **/etc/lightdm/lightdm.conf** file or the files within the **/etc/lightdm/lightdm.conf.d** directory.

/etc/lightdm

The configuration files for lightdm are located within the **/etc/lightdm** directory. There are a lot of possible configuration settings. For example, the following would configure the display manager to automatically log in the user named bob:

```
[SeatDefaults]
autologin-user=bob
autologin-user-timeout=20
```

## CHAPTER 29

Accessibility

This chapter provides information and commands concerning the following topics:

- Basic knowledge of keyboard accessibility settings (AccessX)
- Basic knowledge of visual settings and themes
- Basic knowledge of assistive technology (AT)
- Sticky/Repeat Keys
- Slow/Bounce/Toggle Keys
- Mouse Keys
- High Contrast/Large Print desktop themes
- Screen Reader
- Braille display
- Screen Magnifier
- On-screen keyboard
- Orca
- GOK
- emacspeak

IMPORTANT NOTE: For the LPIC-1 exam, you will only be asked questions regarding what accessibility features are used for, not how to configure their settings. As a result, that will be the focus of this chapter.

Basic Knowledge of Keyboard Accessibility Settings (AccessX)

AccessX refers to both keyboard and mouse accessibility settings. The **accessx** utility provides a GUI-based tool to modify settings such as sticky keys and mouse keys. See the "Sticky/Repeat Keys," "Slow/Bounce/Toggle Keys," and "Mouse Keys" sections in this chapter for more details.

Basic Knowledge of Visual Settings and Themes

See the "High Contrast/Large Print Desktop Themes" section in this chapter for more details.

Basic Knowledge of Assistive Technology (AT)

Assistive technology (AT) is a term that refers to features of Linux that make it easier for users to work with the system. AT covers a wide range of technologies that assist users with visual, hearing, and dexterity impairments in interfacing with Linux. The rest of the sections in this chapter describe the various assistive technologies in greater detail.

Sticky/Repeat Keys

Often to perform an operation, a user may need to hold down a modifier key (such as the Ctrl key or Alt key) while pressing another key (the action key). This can be difficult for some individuals, so Sticky Keys allow a user to press the modifier key once, followed by the action key. Figure 29.1 demonstrates the Universal Access tool, which allows a user to enable Sticky Keys.

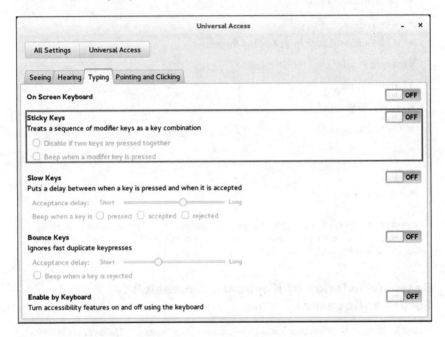

Figure 29.1   Enabling Sticky Keys

Holding down a key on the keyboard may result in multiple characters being generated. For example, if you are in a text editor, holding down the "a" key can result in many *a* characters appearing in a document. Unfortunately, some users tend to have "heavy hands," resulting in multiple characters being typed in situations where that was not the intended result.

By modifying the Repeat Key option, you can increase the length of time that the key must be held down to create multiple characters, thus making it easier for some individuals.

Slow/Bounce/Toggle Keys

Some users tend to press extra keys when moving their fingers from one key to another. The Slow Keys feature can be used to change the keyboard so that a character is not produced unless the user holds down the key for a short period of time.

In some cases, a user may have a shaky hand, resulting in accidently typing a key twice in a row. Bounce Keys is a feature that will ignore duplicate keystrokes. This does, however, require the user to delay typing when double letters are needed.

Ever accidently press the Caps Lock or Num Lock key without realizing it? The Toggle Key feature, when enabled, will emit a sound when a user turns on Caps Lock or Num Lock. Figure 29.2 demonstrates the Universal Access tool, which allows a user to enable Slow Keys and Bounce Keys.

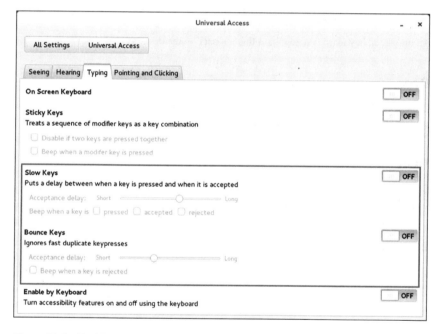

Figure 29.2 Enabling Slow Keys and Bounce Keys

Mouse Keys

This feature allows a user to use the arrow keys on the keyboard to move the mouse arrow on the screen.

High Contrast/Large Print Desktop Themes

A theme modifies the look of your desktop. The High Contrast and Large Print themes are designed for people who have vision impairments.

Screen Reader

Screen Reader is a utility that will read the data from the screen aloud.

Braille Display

A Braille display is essentially a Braille monitor.

Screen Magnifier

Screen Magnifier is a utility that can be used to increase the size of an area of the display.

On-Screen Keyboard

An on-screen keyboard is a keyboard that appears on the desktop.

Orca

Orca is a software tool that acts as an "on-screen" reader. See the "Screen Reader" section in this chapter.

GOK

GOK is an on-screen keyboard provided by GNOME. See the "On-Screen Keyboard" section in this chapter.

emacspeak

emacspeak is a software tool that acts as an "on-screen" reader. See the "Screen Reader" section in this chapter.

## CHAPTER 30

Manage User and Group Accounts and Related System Files

This chapter provides information and commands concerning the following topics:

- Add, modify, and remove users and groups
- Manage user/group info in password/group databases
- Create and manage special-purpose and limited accounts
- /etc/passwd
- /etc/shadow
- /etc/group
- /etc/skel/
- chage
- getent
- groupadd
- groupdel
- groupmod
- passwd
- useradd
- userdel
- usermod

Add, Modify, and Remove Users and Groups

See the "groupadd," "groupmod," "groupdel," "useradd," "usermod," and "userdel" sections in this chapter.

Manage User/Group Info in Password/Group Databases

See the "/etc/passwd," "/etc/shadow," and "/etc/group" sections in this chapter.

Create and Manage Special-Purpose and Limited Accounts

A special-purpose or limited account is an account that has a feature that limits what the user can accomplish on the system. This can include accounts that are only available for a limited time (by setting an expiration date on the password) or application accounts that launch a non-login shell.

For example, suppose there was an interactive tool called **payroll_report** that you wanted a payroll specialist to run using a special-purpose account. You can create this account and then modify the login shell field of the **/etc/password** file to look like the following:

```
rpt:x:50000:50000:payroll report:/home/rpt:/opt/bin/payroll_report
```

When the rpt user logs in, only the **/opt/bin/payroll_report** program is executed.

/etc/passwd

The **/etc/passwd** file is used to store user account information. It contains most of the user account data, except the password and password-aging policies (see the "/etc/shadow" section in this chapter for details about those settings).

Each line in the **/etc/passwd** file describes one user account.

Example:

```
root:x:0:0:root:/root:/bin/bash
```

Every line is broken into fields of data. The following table describes these fields:

Field	Description
User name	**root**:x:0:0:root:/root:/bin/bash This is the name the user will provide when logging in to the system.
Password placeholder	root:**x**:0:0:root:/root:/bin/bash This is the place where the password used to be stored in older versions of Unix.
UID	root:x:**0**:0:root:/root:/bin/bash This is the user ID.
GID	root:x:0:**0**:root:/root:/bin/bash This is the user's primary group ID.
GECOS	root:x:0:0:**root**:/root:/bin/bash GECOS stands for General Electric Comprehensive Operating System; it's typically the user's real name and other identifying data.
Home directory	root:x:0:0:root:**/root**:/bin/bash This is the user's home directory.
Login shell	root:x:0:0:root:/root:**/bin/bash** This is the user's login shell.

/etc/shadow

The **/etc/shadow** file is used to store user password information (see the "/etc/passwd" section in this chapter for details about other user account data).

Each line in the **/etc/shadow** file describes one user account. Here's an example of an account with a valid password:

```
student:$6$ciPSOxID$E5p6cgsPs2lng7dQjrVMIUBGhd/dqs49djnCB1h1oGhryfitza-
VGvsODflyNU67uX3uBraVY0GIOO2zaVGeZ/.:17116:0:99999:7:30:17246:
```

Here's an example of an account with a locked password:

```
bob:*LK*:17116:0:99999:7:30:17246:
```

Every line is broken into fields of data. The following table describes these fields:

Field	Description
User name	bob:*LK*:17116:0:99999:7:30:17246:
	This is the user's name, which is matched up to the entry in the **/etc/passwd** file.
Password	bob:***LK***:17116:0:99999:7:30:17246:
	This is the user's password or some locked value. Note that passwords are encrypted.
Last change	bob:*LK*:**17116**:0:99999:7:30:17246:
	This is the number of days since January 1, 1970 and the last time the user's password was changed. It's used by the system for the next three fields.
Min	bob:*LK*:17116:**0**:99999:7:30:17246:
	How many days after a user's password is changed before the user can change his password again.
Max	bob:*LK*:17116:0:**99999**:7:30:17246:
	This is how many days after a user's password is changed before the user must change his password again. If the user doesn't change his password before this time limit, then the account is locked.
Warn	bob:*LK*:17116:0:99999:**7**:30:17246:
	This is how many days before the account is to be locked to start issuing warnings to the user as the user logs in.
Inactive	bob:*LK*:17116:0:99999:7:**30**:17246:
	After the account is locked, this is how many "grace days" the user has in which he can log in—but only if a new password is provided at login.

Field	Description
Expiration date	bob:*LK*:17116:0:99999:7:30:**17246**: This is the number of days since January 1, 1970 when the user's account will expire.
Unused	bob:*LK*:17116:0:99999:7:30:17246: This is an unused field that may be used in the future.

/etc/group

The **/etc/group** file is used to store group account information. Each line in the **/etc/group** file describes one group account.

Example:

```
admin:x:110:bob,sue
```

Every line is broken into fields of data. The following table describes these fields:

Field	Description
Group name	**admin**:x:110:bob,sue This is the name of the group.
Password placeholder	admin:**x**:110:bob,sue This is the place where the password used to be stored in older versions of Unix.
GID	admin:x:**110**:bob,sue This is the group ID.
Member list	admin:x:110:**bob,sue** These are the members of the group.

/etc/skel/

The **/etc/skel** directory is used when a new user account is created to provide the new account with default files, such as bash configuration files (**.bashrc**, **.profile**, and so on). See the "useradd" section in this chapter for additional details.

chage

The **chage** command is executed by the root user to modify password-aging features for a user account. Important options for the **chage** command include the following:

Option	Description
-d	Change the Last Change field of the **/etc/shadow** file for the user.
-E	Set the Expiration Date field of the **/etc/shadow** file for the user (for example, **chage -E 2025-01-01 bob**).

Option	Description
-m	Change the Min field of the **/etc/shadow** file for the user.
-M	Change the Max field of the **/etc/shadow** file for the user.
-W	Change the Warn field of the **/etc/shadow** file for the user.

See the "/etc/shadow" section in this chapter for additional information regarding password-aging settings.

getent

One use of the **getent** command is to list values that are stored in user and group account databases. For example, to list information about the root user, execute the following command:

```
[root@localhost ~]$ getent passwd root
root:x:0:0:root:/root:/bin/bash
```

groupadd

The **groupadd** command is used by the root user to create a group account.

Example:

```
[root@localhost ~]$ groupadd -g 2050 test
```

The **-g** option is used to specify the GID for the new group.

groupdel

The **groupdel** command is used by the root user to delete a group account.

Example:

```
[root@localhost ~]$ groupdel test
```

> **IMPORTANT NOTE:** Be sure to remove all files owned by the group before running this command (or reassign the files to another group).

groupmod

The **groupmod** command is used by the root user to modify a group account.

Example:

```
[root@localhost ~]$ groupmod -n proj test
```

Important options for the **groupmod** command include the following:

Option	Description
-g	Change the GID.
-n	Change the group name.

passwd

The **passwd** command allows a user to change her password. The root user can also use this command to change any user password or change other password-based features for a user account. Important options for the **passwd** command include the following:

Option	Description
-d	Delete the user's password.
-e	Expire the user account immediately.
-l	Lock the account.
-u	Unlock the account.
-m	Change the Min field of the **/etc/shadow** file for the user.
-M	Change the Max field of the **/etc/shadow** file for the user.
-w	Change the Warn field of the **/etc/shadow** file for the user.

useradd

The **useradd** command is used by the root user to create a user account.

Example:

```
[root@localhost ~]$ useradd julia
```

Important options for the **useradd** command include the following:

Option	Description
-c	Set the comment or GECOS field for the user.
-d	Specify the home directory for the user. This is often used with the **-m** option, which is used to create the home directory.
-e	Set the account's Expiration Date value (see the "/etc/shadow" section in this chapter for more details).
-f	Set the account's Inactive value (see the "/etc/shadow" section in this chapter for more details).
-g	Specify the user's primary group.
-G	Specify the user's secondary groups.
-k	Specify the skel directory; this is the directory from where files are copied automatically into the user's home directory.
-s	Specify the user's login shell.
-u	Specify the user's UID.

userdel

The **userdel** command is used by the root user to delete a user account.

Example:

```
[root@localhost ~]$ userdel susan
```

An important option for the **userdel** command is the **-r** option, which deletes the user account as well has the user's home directory and mail spool.

usermod

The **usermod** command is used by the root user to modify a user account.

Example:

```
[root@localhost ~]$ usermod -s /bin/tcsh julia
```

The **usermod** command uses many of the same options as the **useradd** command. See the "useradd" section in this chapter for a list of these options.

## CHAPTER 31

Automate System Administration Tasks by Scheduling Jobs

This chapter provides information and commands concerning the following topics:

- Manage cron and at jobs
- Configure user access to cron and at services
- Configure anacron
- **/etc/cron.{d,daily,hourly,monthly,weekly}/**
- **/etc/at.deny**
- **/etc/at.allow**
- **/etc/crontab**
- **/etc/cron.allow**
- **/etc/cron.deny**
- **/var/spool/cron/**
- **crontab**
- **at**
- **atq**
- **atrm**
- **anacron**
- **/etc/anacrontab**

Manage cron and at Jobs

See the "crontab," "at," "atq," and "atrm" sections in this chapter for details.

Configure User Access to cron and at Services

As the administrator, you can use configuration files to determine whether a user can use the **crontab** or **at** commands. The **/etc/at.deny** and **/etc/at.allow** files are used to control access to the **at** command, while the **/etc/cron.deny** and **/etc/cron.allow** files are used to control access to the **crontab** command.

The format of each of these files is one username per line. Here's an example:

```
[root@localhost ~]$ cat /etc/at.deny
alias
backup
bin
daemon
ftp
games
gnats
guest
irc
lp
mail
man
nobody
operator
proxy
sync
sys
www-data
```

The following table describes how the **/etc/at.deny** and **/etc/at.allow** files work:

Situation	Description
Only the **/etc/at.deny** file exists.	All users listed in this file are denied access to the **at** command, whereas all other users can execute the **at** command successfully. Use this file when you want to deny access to a few users but allow access to most users.
Only the **/etc/at.allow** file exists.	All users listed in this file are allowed access to the **at** command, whereas all other users cannot execute the **at** command successfully. Use this file when you want to allow access to a few users but deny access to most users.
Neither file exists.	On most Linux distributions, this means that only the root user can use the **at** command. However, on some platforms, this results in all users being allowed to use the **at** command.
Both files exist.	Only the **/etc/at.allow** file is consulted, and the **/etc/at.deny** file is completely ignored.

The following table describes how the **/etc/cron.deny** and **/etc/cron.allow** files work (note: they work the same as the **/etc/at.deny** and **/etc/at.allow** files):

Situation	Description
Only the **/etc/ cron.deny** file exists.	All users listed in this file are denied access to the **crontab** command, whereas all other users can execute the **crontab** command successfully. Use this file when you want to deny access to a few users but allow access to most users.
Only the **/etc/ cron.allow** file exists.	All users listed in this file are allowed access to the **crontab** command, whereas all other users cannot execute the **crontab** command successfully. Use this file when you want to allow access to a few users but deny access to most users.
Neither file exists.	On most Linux distributions, this means that only the root user can use the **crontab** command. However, on some platforms, this results in all users being allowed to use the **crontab** command.
Both files exist.	Only the **/etc/cron.allow** file is consulted, and the **/etc /cron.deny** file is completely ignored.

Configure anacron

See the "anacron" and "/etc/anacron" sections in this chapter for details.

/etc/cron.{d,daily,hourly,monthly,weekly}/

The following table describes these directories: ·

Directory	Description
/etc/cron.d	Location for additional system crontab configurations. The primary system crontab configuration is in **/etc/crontab**, but additional system crontabs can be placed in this directory. See the "/etc/crontab" section in this chapter for additional details.
/etc/cron.daily	This directory contains scripts that will be executed once per day.
/etc/cron.hourly	This directory contains scripts that will be executed every hour.
/etc/ cron.monthly	This directory contains scripts that will be executed once per month.
/etc/cron.weekly	This directory contains scripts that will be executed once per week.

/etc/at.deny

The **/etc/at.deny** file contains a list of users who are not allowed to use the **at** command. See the "Configure User Access to cron and at services" section in this chapter for additional details.

/etc/at.allow

The **/etc/at.allow** file contains a list of users who are allowed to use the **at** command. See the "Configure User Access to cron and at services" section in this chapter for additional details.

/etc/crontab

The **/etc/crontab** file acts as the system crontab. The system administrator edits this file to enable the execution of system-critical processes at specific intervals. The following is a sample **/etc/crontab** file:

```
[root@localhost ~]$ cat /etc/crontab
SHELL=/bin/sh
PATH=/usr/local/sbin:/usr/local/bin:/sbin:/bin:/usr/sbin:/usr/bin

# m h dom mon dow user   command
17 *    * * *    root    cd / && run-parts /etc/cron.hourly
```

Each configuration line describes a process to execute, when to execute it, and what username to execute the process as. Each line is broken into fields, separated by one or more space characters. The following table describes these fields:

Field	Description
First field: Minute	The minute that the command should execute. Values can be from 0–59. A single value can be used or a list of values, such as 0,15,30,45. Range values (1–15) can also be used. An * character means "all possible values."
Second field: Hour	The hour that the command should execute. Values can be from 0–23. A single value can be used or a list of values, such as 0,6,12,18. Range values (8–16) can also be used. An * character means "all possible values."
Third field: Day of the Month	The day of the month that the command should execute. Values can be from 1–31. A single value can be used or a list of values, such as 1,15. Range values (1–10) can also be used. An * character means "not specified," unless the fifth field is also an * character, in which case the * character means "all possible values."
Fourth field: Month	The month that the command should execute. Values can be from 1–12. A single value can be used or a list of values, such as 6,12. Range values (1–3) can also be used. An * character means "all possible values."

Field	Description
Fifth field: Day of the Week	The day of the week that the command should execute. Values can be from 0–7 (0=Sunday, 1=Monday… 6=Saturday, 7=Sunday). A single value can be used or a list of values, such as 1,3,5. Range values (1–5) can also be used. An * character means "not specified," unless the third field is also an * character, in which case the * character means "all possible values."
Sixth field: Username	The name of the user that the command should run as.
Seventh field: Command Name	The name of the command to execute.

/etc/cron.allow

The **/etc/cron.allow** file contains a list of users who are allowed to use the **crontab** command. See the "Configure User Access to cron and at Services" section in this chapter for additional details.

/etc/cron.deny

The **/etc/cron.deny** file contains a list of users who are not allowed to use the **crontab** command. See the "Configure User Access to cron and at Services" section in this chapter for additional details.

/var/spool/cron/

This directory, which can only be viewed by the root user, contains all user **crontab** entries. Each file in this directory will be named after the user who created the **crontab** entry.

The files in this directory are rarely ever modified. Users use the **crontab** command to modify the content of these files. See the "crontab" section in this chapter for additional details.

crontab

The **crontab** command allows a user to view or modify her crontab file. The crontab file allows a user to schedule a command to be executed on a regular basis, such as once an hour or twice a month.

Important options for the **crontab** command include the following:

Option	Description
-e	Edit the crontab file.
-l	List the crontab file.
-r	Remove all entries in the crontab file.

Each line of the crontab file is broken into fields, separated by one or more space characters. The following table describes these fields:

Field	Description
First field: Minute	The minute that the command should execute. Values can be from 0–59. A single value can be used or a list of values, such as 0,15,30,45. Range values (1–15) can also be used. An * character means "all possible values."
Second field: Hour	The hour that the command should execute. Values can be from 0–23. A single value can be used or a list of values, such as 0,6,12,18. Range values (8–16) can also be used. An * character means "all possible values."
Third field: Day of the Month	The day of the month the command should execute. Values can be from 1–31. A single value can be used or a list of values, such as 1,15. Range values (1–10) can also be used. An * character means "not specified," unless the fifth field is also an * character, in which case the * character means "all possible values."
Fourth field: Month	The month that the command should execute. Values can be from 1–12. A single value can be used or a list of values, such as 6,12. Range values (1–3) can also be used. An * character means "all possible values."
Fifth field: Day of the Week	The day of the week that the command should execute. Values can be from 0–7 (0=Sunday, 1=Monday... 6=Saturday, 7=Sunday). A single value can be used or a list of values, such as 1,3,5. Range values (1–5) can also be used. An * character means "not specified," unless the third field is also an * character, in which case the * character means "all possible values."
Sixth field: Command Name	The name of the command to execute.

For example, the following crontab entry will execute the **/home/bob/rpt.pl** script every weekday (Monday–Friday) every month starting at 08:00 in the morning and every half hour until 16:30 in the afternoon (4:30 p.m.):

```
0,30 8-16 * 1-12 1-5 /home/bob/rpt.pl
```

at

The **at** command is used to schedule one or more commands to be executed at one specific time in the future. The syntax for the command is **at** *time*, where *time* indicates when you want to execute a command. For example, the following will allow you to schedule a command to run at 5 p.m. tomorrow:

```
at 5pm tomorrow
at>
```

When provided the **at>** prompt, enter a command to execute at the specified time. To execute multiple commands, press the Enter key for another **at>** prompt.

When this is complete, hold down the CONTROL button and press the d key. That results in a <EOT> message and creates the at job. Here's an example:

```
[root@localhost ~]$ at 5pm tomorrow
at> /home/bob/rpt.pl
at> echo "report complete" | mail bob
at> <EOT>
job 1 at Thu Feb 23 17:00:00 2017
```

atq

The **atq** command lists the current user's at jobs:

```
[root@localhost ~]$ atq
1        Thu Feb 23 17:00:00 2017 a bob
```

The output includes a job number (1 in this example), the date that the command will execute, and the user name (bob in this example).

atrm

To remove an at job before it is executed, run the **atrm** command followed by the job number to remove.

Example:

```
[root@localhost ~]$ atq
1        Thu Feb 23 17:00:00 2017 a bob
[root@localhost ~]$ atrm 1
~/shared$ atq
```

anacron

One issue with the system crontab (the **/etc/crontab** file and the files in the **/etc/cron.d** directory) is what happens when the system is turned off and a command is supposed to be executed. Important system commands can be skipped in situations like this.

The **anacron** command is executed automatically at boot and is designed to execute any commands that were missed while the system was off. It uses the **/etc/anacrontab** file for its configuration.

See the "/etc/anacrontab" section in this chapter for details on this configuration file.

NOTE: On many modern Linux distributions, the **anacron** command has been made obsolete because the modern **crond** daemon handles this function.

/etc/anacrontab

The **/etc/anacrontab** file is used by the **anacron** command to determine how to execute commands that were missed by the **crond** daemon while a system was shut down. A typical **/etc/anacrontab** file looks like this:

```
[root@localhost ~]$ cat /etc/anacrontab
SHELL=/bin/sh
PATH=/sbin:/bin:/usr/sbin:/usr/bin
MAILTO=root
# the maximal random delay added to the base delay of the jobs
RANDOM_DELAY=45
# the jobs will be started during the following hours only
START_HOURS_RANGE=3-22
#period in days   delay in minutes   job-identifier   command
1                 5                   cron.daily       nice run-parts /etc/cron.daily
7                 25                  cron.weekly      nice run-parts /etc/cron.weekly
@monthly          45                  cron.monthly     nice run-parts /etc/cron.monthly
```

The lines at the bottom of this file describe what commands to run and when to run them. Each line is broken into fields, separated by one or more space characters. The following table describes these fields:

Field	Description
First field: Period	The **anacron** command looks in the log files to determine the last time the command listed in the third field was executed. The first field means "if it has been more than this number of days since the last time that command was executed, then execute the command after the boot process has completed."
Second field: Wait Time	Wait this period of time (in minutes) after the system is completed booting before executing the command in the fourth field.

Field	Description
Third field: Command Name	The name of the command that was skipped.
Third field: Command to Execute	The command that should be executed.

Therefore, the following line means "execute the **nice run-parts /etc/cron.daily** command five minutes after the system boots if it has been one day or more since the last time the **cron.daily** command was executed":

```
1        5              cron.daily        nice run-parts /etc/cron.daily
```

## CHAPTER 32

Localization and Internationalization

This chapter provides information and commands concerning the following topics:

- Configure locale settings and environment variables
- Configure timezone settings and environment variables
- **/etc/timezone**
- **/etc/localtime**
- **/usr/share/zoneinfo/**
- **LC_***
- **LC_ALL**
- **LANG**
- **TZ**
- **/usr/bin/locale**
- **tzselect**
- **timedatectl**
- **date**
- **iconv**
- UTF-8
- ISO-8859
- ASCII
- Unicode

Configure Locale Settings and Environment Variables

See the "LC_*," "LC_ALL," "LANG," and "/usr/bin/locale" sections in this chapter.

Configure Timezone Settings and Environment Variables

See the "/etc/timezone," "/etc/localtime," "/usr/share/zoneinfo/," "TZ," "tzselect," "timedatectl," and "date" sections in this chapter.

/etc/timezone

This is the location of the system timezone on Debian-based systems:

```
[root@localhost ~]# more /etc/timezone
America/Los_Angeles
```

This file can be modified manually by using the output of the **tzselect** command. See the "tzselect" section in this chapter for more information.

/etc/localtime

On Red Hat–based distributions, the system timezone is set by the **/etc/localtime** file. This file is a symbolic link to a binary timezone file:

```
[root@localhost ~]# ls -l /etc/localtime
lrwxrwxrwx 1 root root 41 Feb 18  2015 /etc/localtime ->
../usr/share/zoneinfo/America/Los_Angeles
[root@localhost ~]# file /usr/share/zoneinfo/America/Los_Angeles
/usr/share/zoneinfo/America/Los_Angeles: timezone data, version 2,
4 gmt time flags, 4 std time flags, no leap seconds,
185 transition times, 4 abbreviation chars
```

To change the timezone on a system that uses the **/etc/localtime** file, create a new symbolic link:

```
[root@localhost ~]# rm /etc/localtime
[root@localhost ~]# ln -s /usr/share/zoneinfo/America/Goose_Bay /etc/
localtime
[root@localhost ~]# ls -l /etc/localtime
lrwxrwxrwx 1 root root 36 Feb 28  2017 /etc/localtime ->
../usr/share/zoneinfo/America/Goose_Bay
```

/usr/share/zoneinfo/

This directory contains a list of all zone files, either directly in the directory or within subdirectories:

```
[root@localhost ~]# ls /usr/share/zoneinfo
Africa      Chile     GB          Indian      MST        PRC        UTC
America     CST6CDT   GB-Eire     Iran        MST7MDT    PST8PDT    WET
Antarctica  Cuba      GMT         iso3166.tab Navajo     right      W-SU
Arctic      EET       GMT0        Israel      NZ         ROC        zone.tab
Asia        Egypt     GMT-0       Jamaica     NZ-CHAT    ROK        Zulu
Atlantic    Eire      GMT+0       Japan       Pacific    Singapore
Australia   EST       Greenwich   Kwajalein   Poland     Turkey
Brazil      EST5EDT   Hongkong    Libya       Portugal   UCT
Canada      Etc       HST         MET         posix      Universal
CET         Europe    Iceland     Mexico      posixrules US
```

The files within this directory are used to specific the system timezone. See the "/etc/localtime" section in this chapter for more information.

LC_*

LC_* refers to a collection of locale settings that are used to change the way the shell and other programs handle differences based on the geographic region of the user (or a region the user is familiar with). These values can be viewed by executing the **locale** command:

```
[root@localhost ~]# locale
LANG=en_US.UTF-8
LANGUAGE=en_US
LC_CTYPE="en_US.UTF-8"
LC_NUMERIC="en_US.UTF-8"
LC_TIME="en_US.UTF-8"
LC_COLLATE="en_US.UTF-8"
LC_MONETARY="en_US.UTF-8"
LC_MESSAGES="en_US.UTF-8"
LC_PAPER="en_US.UTF-8"
LC_NAME="en_US.UTF-8"
LC_ADDRESS="en_US.UTF-8"
LC_TELEPHONE="en_US.UTF-8"
LC_MEASUREMENT="en_US.UTF-8"
LC_IDENTIFICATION="en_US.UTF-8"
LC_ALL=
```

The more important settings are described in the following table:

Setting	Description
LANG	See the "LANG" section in this chapter.
LC_CTYPE	Case conversion.
LC_NUMERIC	Numeric formats.
LC_TIME	Time and date formats.
LC_COLLATE	Collation order.
LC_MONETARY	Currency formats.
LC_MESSAGES	Format of messages.
LC_PAPER	Paper size formats.
LC_NAME	Name formats.
LC_ADDRESS	Address formats.
LC_TELEPHONE	Telephone formats.
LC_ALL	See the "LC_All" section in this chapter.

Use the **locale -a** command to view all available locales.

LC_ALL

When set, **LC_ALL** will override all other locale settings. This provides an easy means to change all locale settings by modifying one environment variable. Typically this is set for a specific command, as shown here:

```
[root@localhost ~]# LC_ALL=es_ES.UTF8 man
```

See the "LC_*" section in this chapter for additional details.

LANG

When set, **LANG** will provide a default locale value. This can be overwritten for specific locale features by setting other locale variables. For example, the following would set the default to Spanish but use the date/time formats for English:

```
[root@localhost ~]# LANG=es_ES.UTF8 LC_TIME=en_US.utf8 man
```

See the "LC_*" section in this chapter for additional details.

TZ

The **TZ** variable can be used to set a different timezone than the system default:

```
[root@localhost ~]# date
Tue Feb 28 21:58:33 PST 2017
[root@localhost ~]# TZ=America/Goose_Bay date
Wed Mar  1 01:59:02 AST 2017
```

See the "/etc/timezone," "/etc/localtime," and "/usr/share/zoneinfo/" sections in this chapter for more details regarding system timezones.

/usr/bin/locale

See the "LC_*" section for information regarding the **locale** command.

tzselect

The **tzselect** utility is a menu-driven, CLI-based tool that allows a user to select a timezone. The following is a sample execution:

```
[root@localhost ~]# tzselect
Please identify a location so that time zone rules can be set
correctly.
```

Please select a continent, ocean, "coord", or "TZ".

1) Africa

2) Americas

3) Antarctica

4) Arctic Ocean

5) Asia

6) Atlantic Ocean

7) Australia

8) Europe

9) Indian Ocean

10) Pacific Ocean

11) coord - I want to use geographical coordinates.

12) TZ - I want to specify the time zone using the Posix TZ format.

#? **2**

Please select a country whose clocks agree with yours.

1) Anguilla		28) Haiti
2) Antigua & Barbuda		29) Honduras
3) Argentina		30) Jamaica
4) Aruba		31) Martinique
5) Bahamas		32) Mexico
6) Barbados		33) Montserrat
7) Belize		34) Nicaragua
8) Bolivia		35) Panama
9) Brazil		36) Paraguay
10) Canada		37) Peru
11) Caribbean Netherlands		38) Puerto Rico
12) Cayman Islands		39) St Barthelemy
13) Chile		40) St Kitts & Nevis
14) Colombia		41) St Lucia
15) Costa Rica		42) St Maarten (Dutch part)
16) Cuba		43) St Martin (French part)
17) Curacao		44) St Pierre & Miquelon
18) Dominica		45) St Vincent
19) Dominican Republic		46) Suriname
20) Ecuador		47) Trinidad & Tobago
21) El Salvador		48) Turks & Caicos Is
22) French Guiana		49) United States
23) Greenland		50) Uruguay
24) Grenada		51) Venezuela
25) Guadeloupe		52) Virgin Islands (UK)
26) Guatemala		53) Virgin Islands (US)
27) Guyana		

#? **49**

```
Please select one of the following time zone regions.
 1) Eastern Time
 2) Eastern Time - Michigan - most locations
 3) Eastern Time - Kentucky - Louisville area
 4) Eastern Time - Kentucky - Wayne County
 5) Eastern Time - Indiana - most locations
 6) Eastern Time - Indiana - Daviess, Dubois, Knox & Martin Counties
 7) Eastern Time - Indiana - Pulaski County
 8) Eastern Time - Indiana - Crawford County
 9) Eastern Time - Indiana - Pike County
10) Eastern Time - Indiana - Switzerland County
11) Central Time
12) Central Time - Indiana - Perry County
13) Central Time - Indiana - Starke County
14) Central Time - Michigan - Dickinson, Gogebic, Iron & Menominee
Counties
15) Central Time - North Dakota - Oliver County
16) Central Time - North Dakota - Morton County (except Mandan area)
17) Central Time - North Dakota - Mercer County
18) Mountain Time
19) Mountain Time - south Idaho & east Oregon
20) Mountain Standard Time - Arizona (except Navajo)
21) Pacific Time
22) Pacific Standard Time - Annette Island, Alaska
23) Alaska Time
24) Alaska Time - Alaska panhandle
25) Alaska Time - southeast Alaska panhandle
26) Alaska Time - Alaska panhandle neck
27) Alaska Time - west Alaska
28) Aleutian Islands
29) Hawaii
#? 23
The following information has been given:

        United States
        Alaska Time


Therefore TZ='America/Anchorage' will be used.
Local time is now:     Tue Feb 28 21:03:15 AKST 2017.
Universal Time is now: Wed Mar  1 06:03:15 UTC 2017.
Is the above information OK?
1) Yes
2) No
#? 1
```

You can make this change permanent for yourself by appending the line

        TZ='America/Anchorage'; export TZ

to the file '.profile' in your home directory; then log out and log in again.

Here is that TZ value again, this time on standard output so that you can use the /usr/bin/tzselect command in shell scripts:

America/Anchorage

timedatectl

Use the **timedatectl** command to display the system clock:

```
[root@localhost ~]# timedatectl
      Local time: Tue 2017-02-28 22:07:39 PST
  Universal time: Wed 2017-03-01 06:07:39 UTC
        RTC time: Sun 2016-06-12 17:50:56
        Timezone: America/Los_Angeles (PST, -0800)
     NTP enabled: yes
NTP synchronized: no
 RTC in local TZ: no
      DST active: no
 Last DST change: DST ended at
                  Sun 2016-11-06 01:59:59 PDT
                  Sun 2016-11-06 01:00:00 PST
 Next DST change: DST begins (the clock jumps one hour forward) at
                  Sun 2017-03-12 01:59:59 PST
                  Sun 2017-03-12 03:00:00 PDT
```

As the root user, you can use this command to set the system clock. The following table demonstrates the more commonly used methods of changing the system clock:

Method	Description
set-time [*time*]	Sets the system clock to the specified *time*.
set-timezone [*zone*]	Sets the system timezone to the specified *zone*.
set-ntp [**0**|**1**]	Enables (**1**) or disables (**0**) the Network Time Protocol.

date

Use the **date** command to display the system clock:

```
[root@localhost ~]# date
Tue Feb 28 22:15:33 PST 2017
```

The output of the **date** command is commonly used to generate unique filenames because the command has a very flexible output format. Here's an example:

```
[root@localhost ~]# date "+%F"
2017-02-28
[root@localhost ~]# touch data-$(date "+%F")
[root@localhost ~]# ls data*
data-2017-02-28
```

The following table details some of the more commonly used date formats:

Format	Description
%a	Abbreviated weekday name (Sun).
%A	Full weekday name (Sunday).
%b	Abbreviated month (Jan).
%B	Full month (January).
%d	Day of the month.
%D	Same as %m/%d/%y.
%F	Same as %Y-%m-%d.
%m	Month.
%n	A newline character.
%y	Two-digit year.
%Y	Four-digit year.

As the root user, you can use the **date** command to set the system clock using the following syntax:

```
[root@localhost ~]# date Tue Feb 28 22:15:33 PST 2017
```

iconv

The **iconv** command will convert the contents of a file from one format to another. See the "UTF-8," "ISO-8859," "ASCII," and "Unicode" sections in this chapter for more details about encoding formats.

The syntax for the **iconv** command is as follows:

```
iconv -c -f from_format -t to_format input_file > output_file
```

UTF-8

See the "Unicode" section in this chapter.

ISO-8859

An encoding standard that includes ASCII within the first 7 bits (128 characters) and additional characters for the 8th bit. Different variations of ISO-8859 exist. For example, ISO-8859-1 (typically the default Linux character set) is Latin-based (Western European) whereas ISO-8859-14 is Celtic-based.

ASCII

American Standard Code for Information Interchange (ASCII) is an English-only encoding format that is limited to 128 characters (a 7-bit code). Extended ASCII can support additional, non-English characters.

Unicode

An encoding standard that includes ASCII within the first 7 bits (128 characters). The additional bits are used for additional, non-English characters. Unicode has gone through several revisions, including UTF-8, UTF-16, and USC (which is not considered to be obsolete).

## CHAPTER 33

Maintain System Time

This chapter provides information and commands concerning the following topics:

- Set the system date and time
- Set the hardware clock to the correct time in UTC
- Configure the correct timezone
- Basic NTP configuration
- Knowledge of using the **pool.ntp.org** service
- Awareness of the **ntpq** command
- **/usr/share/zoneinfo/**
- **/etc/timezone**
- **/etc/localtime**
- **/etc/ntp.conf**
- **date**
- **hwclock**
- **ntpd**
- **ntpdate**
- **pool.ntp.org**

Set the System Date and Time

See the "hwclock" section in this chapter and the "date" section in Chapter 32, "Localization and Internationalization," for details.

Set the Hardware Clock to the Correct Time in UTC

See the "hwclock" section in this chapter for details.

Configure the Correct Timezone

See the "tzselect" section in Chapter 32 for details.

Basic NTP Configuration

See the "/etc/ntp.conf" section in this chapter for details.

Knowledge of Using the pool.ntp.org Service

See the "pool.ntp.org" section in this chapter for details.

Awareness of the ntpq Command

The **ntpq** command allows you to perform queries on NTP servers:

```
[root@localhost ~]# ntpq -p
     remote           refid      st t when poll reach   delay    offset
jitter
==============================================================
*propjet.latt.ne 68.110.9.223     2 u  120 1024  377    98.580    7.067
4.413
-services.quadra  208.75.88.4     3 u  272 1024  377    72.504  -10.689
1.612
+mirror          216.93.242.12    3 u  287 1024  377    20.406   -2.555
0.822
+108.61.194.85.v 200.23.51.102    2 u  741 1024  377    69.403   -3.670
1.610
```

Important options for the **ntpq** command include the following:

Option	Description
-d	Enable debugging mode.
-n	List host IP addresses rather than names.
-p	Print a list of all peers.

/usr/share/zoneinfo/

See the "/usr/share/zoneinfo/" section in Chapter 32 for information.

/etc/timezone

See the "/etc/timezone" section in Chapter 32 for information.

/etc/localtime

See the "/etc/localtime" section in Chapter 32 for information.

/etc/ntp.conf

The **/etc/ntp.conf** file is the primary configuration file for the **ntpd** service. Important settings include the following:

Option	Description
driftfile	This file contains a value that represents the typical delta (change) over time from the NTP reported time and the system clock. This value is used to regularly update the system clock without having to access an NTP server.
restrict	Used to indicate restrictions for the daemon, including what machines can access this NTP server when it is used as a service.
server	Used to list an NTP server for this machine when it is used as an NTP client.

date

See the "date" section in Chapter 32 for information.

hwclock

The **hwclock** command is used to display the real-time clock (RTC). To view the RTC, execute the **hwclock** command with no arguments:

```
[root@localhost ~]# hwclock
Mon 13 Jun 2016 01:23:32 AM PDT   -0.466658 seconds
```

Important options for the **hwclock** command include the following:

Option	Description
--date	Used with the **--set** option to set the RTC.
--set	Sets the RTC based on the argument provided to the **--date** option.
-s or **--hctosys**	Sets the system time based on the current RTC time.
--systz	Resets the RTC based on the current timezone.
-w or **--systohc**	Sets the RTC time based on the current system time.

ntpd

The Network Time Protocol daemon (ntpd) is a process that ensures the system clock is in sync with the time provided by remote NTP servers. Most of the configuration for this process is handled via the **/etc/ntp.conf** file; however, a few options are sometimes used, as detailed in the following table:

Option	Description
-c *file*	Used to specify an alternative configuration file.
-l *file*	Used to specify a log file location.
-u user:group	Used to specify the user and group to run the ntpd process as.

See the "/etc/ntp.conf" section in this chapter for details on configuring the ntpd service.

ntpdate

The **ntpdate** command is traditionally used to manually set the system time to NTP time; however, on newer systems the ntpd server also provides this functionality.

pool.ntp.org

The **pool.ntp.org** address is a link to a cluster of NTP servers that are geographically spread throughout the world. These servers can be freely used within the **/etc/ntp.conf** file:

```
server 0.pool.ntp.org
server 1.pool.ntp.org
server 2.pool.ntp.org
server 3.pool.ntp.org
```

CHAPTER 34

System Logging

This chapter provides information and commands concerning the following topics:

- Configuration of the syslog daemon
- Understanding of standard facilities, priorities, and actions
- Configuration of **logrotate**
- Awareness of rsyslog and syslog-ng
- **syslog.conf**
- **syslogd**
- **klogd**
- **/var/log/**
- **logger**
- **logrotate**
- **/etc/logrotate.conf**
- **/etc/logrotate.d/**
- **journalctl**
- **/etc/systemd/journald.conf**
- **/var/log/journal/**

Configuration of the Syslog Daemon

See the "syslog.conf" section in this chapter.

Understanding of Standard Facilities, Priorities, and Actions

See the "syslog.conf" section in this chapter.

Configuration of logrotate

See the "logrotate," "/etc/logrotate.conf," and "/etc/logrotate.d/" sections in this chapter.

Awareness of rsyslog and syslog-ng

The syslog service has existed since 1980. Although it was advanced at the time is was created, its limitations have grown over time as more complex logging techniques became required.

In the late 1990s, the syslog-ng service was created to extend the features of the traditional syslog service. Remote logging (including TCP support) was included.

In the mid-2000s, the rsyslog service was created, also as an extension of the traditional syslog service. The rsyslog service includes the ability to extend the capabilities by including modules.

In all three cases, the configuration of the services (the format of the **syslog.conf** file) is consistent, with the exception of slightly different naming conventions (**rsyslog.conf**, for example) and additional features available in the log files.

syslog.conf

The **/etc/syslog.conf** file is one of the configuration files for the **syslogd** daemon. The following demonstrates a typical **syslog.conf** file with the comments and blank lines removed:

```
[root@localhost ~]# grep -v "^$" /etc/syslog.conf | grep -v "^#"
*.info;mail.none;authpriv.none;cron.none        /var/log/messages
authpriv.*                                      /var/log/secure
mail.*                                          -/var/log/maillog
cron.*                                          /var/log/cron
*.emerg                                         *
uucp,news.crit                                  /var/log/spooler
local7.*                                        /var/log/boot.log
```

Every line represents one logging rule that is broken into two primary parts: the selector (for example, **uucp,news.crit**) and action (**/var/log/spooler**). The selector is also broken into two parts: the facility (**uucp,news**) and priority (**crit**).

The following list shows the available facilities:

- auth (or security)
- authpriv
- cron
- daemon
- kern
- lpr
- mail
- mark
- news

- syslog

- user

- uucp

- local0 through local7

The following list shows the available priority levels:

- debug

- info

- notice

- warning (or warn)

- err (or error)

- crit

- alert

- emerg (or panic)

The following list shows the available actions:

- Regular file (using "-" before the filename omits syncing with every log entry, thus reducing hard drive writes).

- Named pipes.

- Console or terminal devices.

- Remote hosts.

- User(s). Writes to the specified user's terminal windows (use * for all users).

syslogd

The **syslogd** daemon is responsible for logging of application and system events. It determines which events to log and where to place log entries by configuration settings that are located in the **/etc/syslog.conf** file.

Important options to the **syslogd** command include the following:

Option	Description
-d	Enable debugging mode.
-f	Specify the configuration file (**/etc/syslog.conf** is the default).
-m x	Create a timestamp in the log files every x minutes. Set this to 0 to omit timestamps.
-r	Enables the **syslogd** daemon to accept logs from remote systems.
-S	Verbose mode.
-x	Disable DNS lookups for IP addresses.

klogd

The **klogd** daemon creates kernel logs. Typically the **klogd** daemon sends log entries to the **syslogd** daemon for parsing. Important options for the **klogd** command include the following:

Option	Description
-d	Enable debugging mode.
-f	Log message to a file rather than send it to the **syslogd** daemon.

/var/log/

The **/var/log** directory is the standard location for log files to be placed by the **syslogd** daemon.

logger

The **logger** utility can be used to send a log entry to the **syslogd** daemon:

```
[root@localhost ~]# logger -p local7.warn "warning"
```

Important options for the **logger** command include the following:

Option	Description
-i	Log the PID of the logger process.
-s	Output message to STDERR as well as send it to the **syslogd** daemon.
-f *file*	Use the contents of *file* as the message to send to the **syslogd** daemon.
-p	Specify the facility and priority.
-t	Mark the log entry with a tag for searching purposes.

logrotate

The **logrotate** command is a utility designed to ensure that the partition that holds the log files has enough room to handle the log files. Log file size increases over time. The **logrotate** command rotates log files over time to limit the filesystem space that the logs use.

This command is configured by the **/etc/logrotate.conf** file and files in the **/etc/logrotate.d** directory. Typically, the **logrotate** command is configured to run automatically as a cron job:

```
[root@localhost ~]# cat /etc/cron.daily/logrotate
#!/bin/sh

/usr/sbin/logrotate /etc/logrotate.conf
EXITVALUE=$?
if [ $EXITVALUE != 0 ]; then
    /usr/bin/logger -t logrotate "ALERT exited abnormally with
[$EXITVALUE]"
fi
exit 0
```

See the "/etc/logrotate.conf" and "/etc/logrotatd.d/" sections in this chapter for details on how to configure the **logrotate** utility.

/etc/logrotate.conf

The **/etc/logrotate.conf** file is the primary configuration file for the **logrotate** command. Here's an example of a typical **/etc/logrotate.conf** file:

```
[root@localhost ~]# cat /etc/logrotate.conf
# see "man logrotate" for details
# rotate log files weekly
weekly

# keep 4 weeks worth of backlogs
rotate 4

# create new (empty) log files after rotating old ones
create

# uncomment this if you want your log files compressed
#compress

# RPM packages drop log rotation information into this directory
include /etc/logrotate.d

# no packages own wtmp -- we'll rotate them here
/var/log/wtmp {
    monthly
    minsize 1M
    create 0664 root utmp
    rotate 1
}
```

The top part of this file is used to enable global settings that apply to all files that are rotated by the **logrotate** utility. These global settings can be overridden for individual files by a section defined like the following:

```
/var/log/wtmp {
    monthly
    minsize 1M
    create 0664 root utmp
    rotate 1
}
```

Typically these sections are found in files located in the **/etc/logrotate.d** directory. See the "/etc/logrotate.d" section in this chapter for additional information.

Important settings in the **/etc/logrotate.conf** file include the following:

Settings	Description
daily|weekly|monthly	How often to rotate files.
rotate x	Keep x number of old (backup) files.
Create	Create a new log file when backing up the old log file.
Compress	Compress the backup log file, using gzip by default; the **compress** command can be changed by the **compress-cmd** setting.
Compresscmd	Specify the compression utility to use when compressing backup log files.
Datetext	Backup log files are normally named by the convention **logfile.x** where x represents a number (0, 1, 2, and so on); using **datetext** will change the extension to a date value (YYYYMMDD).
mail *address*	Mail backup log file to *address*.
minsize x	Only rotate log file if its size is at least the value specified by X.
Nocompress	Do not compress the backup copy of the log file.
olddir *dir*	Place backup log files in the *dir* directory.

/etc/logrotate.d/

Files in this directory are used to override the default settings in the **/etc/logrotate.conf** file for the **logrotate** utility. The settings for these files are the same as the settings for the **/etc/logrotate.conf** file. See the "/etc/logrotate.conf" section in this chapter for details.

journalctl

On modern Linux systems, the logging process is handled by the **systemd-journald** service. To query systemd log entries, use the **journalctl** command:

```
[root@localhost ~]# journalctl | head
-- Logs begin at Tue 2017-01-24 13:43:18 PST, end at Sat 2017-03-04
16:00:32 PST. --
Jan 24 13:43:18 localhost.localdomain systemd-journal[88]: Runtime
journal is using 8.0M (max allowed 194.4M, trying to leave 291.7M free
of 1.8G available → current limit 194.4M).
Jan 24 13:43:18 localhost.localdomain systemd-journal[88]: Runtime
journal is using 8.0M (max allowed 194.4M, trying to leave 291.7M free
of 1.8G available → current limit 194.4M).
Jan 24 13:43:18 localhost.localdomain kernel: Initializing cgroup
subsys cpuset
Jan 24 13:43:18 localhost.localdomain kernel: Initializing cgroup
subsys cpu
Jan 24 13:43:18 localhost.localdomain kernel: Initializing cgroup
subsys cpuacct
Jan 24 13:43:18 localhost.localdomain kernel: Linux version 3.10.0-
327.18.2.el7.x86_64 (builder@kbuilder.dev.centos.org) (gcc version
4.8.3 20140911 (Red Hat 4.8.3-9) (GCC) ) #1 SMP Thu May 12 11:03:55
UTC 2016
Jan 24 13:43:18 localhost.localdomain kernel: Command line: BOOT_
IMAGE=/vmlinuz-3.10.0-327.18.2.el7.x86_64 root=/dev/mapper/centos-root
ro rd.lvm.lv=centos/root rd.lvm.lv=centos/swap crashkernel=auto rhgb
quiet LANG=en_US.UTF-8
Jan 24 13:43:18 localhost.localdomain kernel: e820: BIOS-provided
physical RAM map:
Jan 24 13:43:18 localhost.localdomain kernel: BIOS-e820:
[mem 0x0000000000000000-0x000000000009fbff] usable
```

Important options for the **journalctl** command include the following:

Option	Description
--all or -a	Show all fields in full format.
-r	Reverse the log order so newest entries are displayed first.
-k	Show only kernel messages.
--priority=*value*	Only show messages that match the priority *value* (emerg, alert, crit, err, warning, notice, info, or debug).

/etc/systemd/journald.conf

The **/etc/systemd/journald.conf** file is used to configure the **systemd-journald** service. Typically, this file contains all commented-out values by default. Important settings for the **/etc/systemd/journald.conf** file include the following:

Setting	Description
Storage=*value*	Indicates where to store the journal date; *value* can be **volatile, persistent, auto,** or **none.**
Compress=*[1|0]*	If set to **1** (true), this option indicates compression of journal entries before writing to the file.

/var/log/journal/

This directory is where the **systemd-journald** service stores journal entries if the **Storage=persistent** setting is placed in the **/etc/systemd/journald.conf** file.

## CHAPTER 35

Mail Transfer Agent (MTA) Basics

This chapter provides information and commands concerning the following topics:

- Create email aliases
- Configure email forwarding
- Knowledge of commonly available MTA programs (postfix, sendmail, qmail, exim) (no configuration)
- **newaliases**
- **mail**
- **mailq**
- postfix
- sendmail
- exim
- qmail
- **~/.forward**
- **sendmail** emulation layer commands

Create Email Aliases

See the "newaliases" section in this chapter.

Configure Email Forwarding

See the "~/.forward" section in this chapter.

Knowledge of Commonly Available MTA Programs (postfix, sendmail, qmail, exim) (no configuration)

The LPIC exam requires an understanding of mail servers—also called *mail transfer agents* (MTAs)—but you do not need to know how to configure a mail server. Additionally, that topic is beyond the scope of this book. The following provides a brief summary of the sendmail, postfix, qmail, and exim mail servers:

- **Sendmail**—An older MTA service that predates the creation of Linux, sendmail is not often used on modern Linux distributions. Its configuration is considered by many to be cryptic, yet powerful.

- **Postfix**—A more modern MTA that is commonly found on modern Linux distributions. Considered easier to configure and more flexible than sendmail by many. Instead of a single executable, several processes make up the Postfix MTA service.

- **Qmail**—An MTA designed around security features, qmail uses simple configuration files and separate processes to handle its tasks. Development in this project has been slow recently when compared to postfix.

- **Exim**—Another MTA with advanced security features and ease of configuration. Like sendmail, exim uses a single process for all operations.

newaliases

The **newaliases** command converts mail aliases found in the **/etc/aliases** file and converts them into a database used by the mail server. The format of the **/etc/aliases** file is one alias per line; for example, *alias_name: recipient*.

Example:

```
[root@localhost ~]# tail /etc/aliases
marketing:      postmaster
sales:          postmaster
support:        postmaster


# trap decode to catch security attacks
decode:         root

# Person who should get root's mail
#root:          marc
```

There are no options for the **newaliases** command; just modify the **/etc/aliases** file and then run the **newaliases** command.

mail

The **mail** command (**mailx** on some distributions) is a command-line *mail user agent* (MUA). It can be used to send email on the command line, as shown here:

```
mail user@domain
```

Important options for the **mail** command include the following:

Option	Description
-s	Provide a subject line for the mail message.
-a	Add an attachment (not supported by all **mail** commands).
-c	Provide a CC (carbon copy) address.

Option	Description
-b	Provide a BCC (blind carbon copy) address.
-r	Specify the "from" address.

When used with no arguments, the **mail** command can also be used to read the mail for the current user.

mailq

The **mailq** command is used to display the current mail queue (mail messages waiting to be sent by the mail server). To view the queue, run the command with no arguments, like so:

```
[root@localhost ~]# mailq
-Queue ID- --Size-- ----Arrival Time---- -Sender/Recipient-------
64880118DE4D*    446 Sat Mar  4 16:38:59  root@server.sample999.com
                                          bob@host.com

-- 0 Kbytes in 1 Request.
```

postfix

See the "Knowledge of Commonly Available MTA Programs (postfix, sendmail, qmail, exim) (no configuration)" section in this chapter.

sendmail

See the "Knowledge of Commonly Available MTA Programs (postfix, sendmail, qmail, exim) (no configuration)" section in this chapter.

exim

See the "Knowledge of Commonly Available MTA Programs (postfix, sendmail, qmail, exim) (no configuration)" section in this chapter.

qmail

See the "Knowledge of Commonly Available MTA Programs (postfix, sendmail, qmail, exim) (no configuration)" section in this chapter.

~/.forward

Individual users can create a **.forward** file in their home directory to have mail messages that are sent to the account forwarded to another account. For example, the following would forward all incoming messages for the user bob to the account test@test.com:

```
[bob@localhost ~]# cat .forward
test@test.com
```

By default, forwarded mail will not show up in the local user's mail queue unless the
.forward file includes the user's name with a backslash (\) character. This keeps a local
copy of all forwarded email on the system:

```
[bob@localhost ~]# cat .forward
\bob
test@test.com
```

sendmail Emulation Layer Commands

Because sendmail has been popular for so long, postfix provided similar commands to
newaliases and **mailq** to emulate the functionality that these commands provide:

- **postqueue -p** is the emulation command for the **mailq** command.
- **postalias /etc/postfix/aliases** is the emulation command for the newaliases
  command.

## CHAPTER 36

Manage Printers and Printing

This chapter provides information and commands concerning the following topics:

- Basic CUPS configuration (for local and remote printers)
- Manage user print queues
- Troubleshoot general printing problems
- Add and remove jobs from configured printer queues
- CUPS configuration files, tools, and utilities
- /etc/cups/
- lpd legacy interface (**lpr, lprm, lpq**)

Basic CUPS Configuration (for Local and Remote Printers)

The Common Unix Printing System (CUPS) can be configured via command-line tools, a web-based interface, or (depending on your distribution) a GUI-based tool. Because of the nature of the LPIC multiple-choice exam, the questions focus on the command-line tools.

To create a printer, use the **lpadmin** command, as shown here:

```
lpadmin -p printer_name -E -v device_name
```

Important options for the **lpadmin** command include the following:

Option	Description
-p	Used to specify the name of the printer.
-E	Enables the printer and sets the print queue to accept mode.
-v	Used to specify the device name (called the **device-uri**); use the following device name for a remote printer: **socket://** *IP_address*.
-d	Sets the system default printer.
-x	Deletes the printer.

Some CUPS configuration can be performed by executing the **cupsctl** command. By default, it displays the current settings:

```
[root@localhost ~]# cupsctl
_debug_logging=1
_remote_admin=0
_remote_any=0
_share_printers=0
_user_cancel_any=0
BrowseLocalProtocols=dnssd
DefaultAuthType=Basic
JobPrivateAccess=default
JobPrivateValues=default
MaxLogSize=0
SubscriptionPrivateAccess=default
SubscriptionPrivateValues=default
WebInterface=Yes
```

The following table describes the important settings that can be made with the **cupsctl** command and associated files:

File	Description
_debug_logging	Enable (**--debug-logging**) or disable (**--no-debug-logging**) debugging mode for more or fewer log messages.
_remote_admin	Allow (**--remote-admin**) or disallow (**--no-remote-admin**) remote access to the administration features of CUPS.
_remote_any	Allow (**--remote-any**) or disallow (**--no-remote-any**) remote access to the CUPS service from the Internet (remote systems).
_share_printers	Automatically share printers (**--share-printers**) or don't share printers (**--no-share-printers**).
_user_cancel_any	Allow (**--user-cancel-any**) or disallow (**--no-user-cancel-any**) users to cancel any print job (disallowing still permits a user to cancel her own print job).

Manage User Print Queues

A printer that is ready to print is considered to be accepting print requests and is enabled. You can block print requests from being sent to the print queue by executing the following command:

```
cupsreject printer
```

When a printer is rejecting, the print jobs in the queue are still sent to the printer, but no new print jobs will be sent to the print queue. When you're using the **cupsreject** command, use the **-r** option to provide a reason for rejecting jobs:

```
cupsreject -r "printer down for repairs" printer
```

To allow print jobs to be sent to the printer, use the following command:

```
cupsaccept printer
```

In some cases, you may want to stop print jobs from going from the print queue to the printer. This may be for a quick repair, such as a paper jam. To stop print jobs from being sent to the printer, use the following command:

```
cupsdisable printer
```

Users can still print to the print queue as long as the printer is in accept mode. To allow print jobs to go from the queue to the printer, use the following command:

```
cupsenable printer
```

The following demonstrates the difference between accept/reject versus enable/disable:

```
print request -> [accept|reject] -> print queue -> [enable|disable] -> printer
```

Troubleshoot General Printing Problems

The following are a few techniques (presented in order) you can use to troubleshoot printer issues:

1. Check the printer for problems (out of paper, printer jam, and so on).

2. Check the connection to the printer.

3. Attempt to send a simple print job to the print queue (use the **lpr** command).

4. View the print queue.

5. Look at the status of the printer to ensure it is enabled and the print queue is accepting print requests.

6. Restart the CUPS service (this technique varies depending on whether your distribution uses SysVinit, Upstart, or Systemd).

7. View the CUPS error log.

8. Enable debugging mode by choosing "Debugging Information for Troubleshooting" in the Administration section of the CUPS Web UI or use the **cupsctl** command **cupsctl --debug-logging**.

Add and Remove Jobs from Configured Printer Queues

See the **lpr** and **lprm** commands in the "lpd Legacy Interface (lpr, lprm, lpq)" section in this chapter.

CUPS Configuration Files, Tools, and Utilities

See the "Basic CUPS Configuration (for Local and Remote Printers)" and "Manage User Print Queues" sections in this chapter.

/etc/cups/

The **/etc/cups** directory is the location of the CUPS configuration files. The following table describes these files:

File	Description
classes.conf	Defines printer classes (collections of printers).
cupsd.conf	The primary configuration file for the CUPS service.
printers.conf	The configuration file that defines the printers configured on the system.

lpd Legacy Interface (lpr, lprm, lpq)

Although the CUPS commands can handle all the printing tasks for modern Linux distributions, older printer commands are still available:

- **lpr**—A command-line tool to send print jobs to the printer. Syntax: **lpr -P** *printer_name file_to_print*.

- **lpq**—A command-line tool that displays the status of a printer. Use the **-a** option to display the status of all printers.

- **lprm**—A command-line tool that removes print jobs from the print queue.

## CHAPTER 37

Fundamentals of Internet Protocols

This chapter provides information and commands concerning the following topics:

- Demonstrate an understanding of network masks and CIDR notation
- Knowledge of the differences between private and public "dotted quad" IP addresses
- Knowledge about common TCP and UDP ports and services (20, 21, 22, 23, 25, 53, 80, 110, 123, 139, 143, 161, 162, 389, 443, 465, 514, 636, 993, 995)
- Knowledge about the differences and major features of UDP, TCP, and ICMP
- Knowledge of the major differences between IPv4 and IPv6
- Knowledge of the basic features of IPv6
- **/etc/services**
- IPv4, IPv6
- Subnetting
- TCP, UDP, ICMP

Demonstrate an Understanding of Network Masks and CIDR Notation

An IPv4 address consists of four numbers separated by a dot character (for example, 192.168.100.25). Each number represents an octet, a number that can also be represented by a binary value:

11000000.10101000.01100100.00011001

For example, 192 can be represented by the binary number 11000000 because each binary value represents a numeric value, as shown in Figure 37.1.

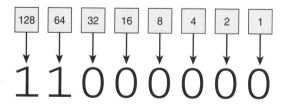

Figure 37.1   Binary Representation of a Numeric Value

The following table describes the standard IPv4 address classes:

Class	Description
A	Ranges from 1.x.x.x to 126.x.x.x. Allows for 127 networks, each with up to 16 million hosts. The first octet defines the network address and the remaining octets define the host addresses.
B	Ranges from 128.x.x.x to 191.x.x.x. Allows for approximately 16,000 networks, each with up to 65,000 hosts.
C	Ranges from 192.x.x.x to 223.x.x.x. Allows for approximately 2 million networks, each with up to 254 million hosts.
D	Only used for multicast groups.
E	Only used for research and development.

Organizations that have been assigned large networks (class A or B, although even class C networks apply here) don't want to have millions or even thousands of hosts on a single network. *Subnetting* provides a method of breaking large network into smaller sections.

The following table demonstrates how the subnet value of 255.255.240 (or 28 using CIDR notation) is applied to the address 192.168.100.25:

Address	192.168.100.25	11000000.10101000.01100100.00011001
Netmask	255.255.255.240 = 28	11111111.11111111.11111111.00010000
Network	192.168.100.16/28	11000000.10101000.01100100.00010000
Broadcast	192.168.100.31	11000000.10101000.01100100.00011111
First IP	192.168.100.17	11000000.10101000.01100100.00010001
Last IP	192.168.100.30	11000000.10101000.01100100.00011110
Hosts in network	14	

Knowledge of the Differences Between Private and Public "Dotted Quad" IP Addresses

Private IP networks use IP addresses in any of the following ranges:

- 192.168.0.0–192.168.255.255
- 172.16.0.0–172.31.255.255
- 10.0.0.0–10.255.255.255

All other valid class A, B or C addresses are considered public IP addresses, except the following:

- The 127.0.0.0–127.255.255.255 range, which is the loopback address range for the local host

- The 0.0.0.0–0.255.255.255 range, which is used to broadcast messages locally

- The 198.51.100.0–198.51.100.255 and 203.0.113.0–203.0.113.255 ranges, which have been assigned for documentation and testing and should never be used publically

Knowledge About Common TCP and UDP Ports and Services (20, 21, 22, 23, 25, 53, 80, 110, 123, 139, 143, 161, 162, 389, 443, 465, 514, 636, 993, 995)

The following table lists the usage for common TCP and UDP ports and services:

Port	Service
20 and 21	FTP
22	SSH
23	Telnet
25	SMTP
53	DNS
80	HTTP
110	POP3
123	NTP
139	NetBIOS
143	IMAP
161 and 162	SNMP
389	LDAP
443	HTTPS
465	SMTPS
514	syslog
636	LDAPS
993	IMAPS
995	POP3S

NOTE: For the LPIC-1 exam, you should memorize these ports and services. In real life, you can always refer to the **/etc/services** file. See the "/etc/services" section in this chapter for more information about this file.

Knowledge About the Differences and Major Features of UDP, TCP, and ICMP

The following table describes the differences between and major features of UDP, TCP, and ICMP:

Protocol	Description
UDP	User Datagram Protocol.
	Complements IP (Internet Protocol).
	Data packages are connectionless, which means no error checking is performed to determine if packages are lost in transmission.
	Faster than TCP because connectionless data transfer requires less "work."
	Less reliable than TCP because of the lack of error checking.
	Example use: live streaming of video in which the loss of an occasional package doesn't have any major impact on the overall data flow.
TCP	Transmission Control Protocol.
	Complements IP (Internet Protocol).
	Data packages are "connection-based," which means error checking is performed to determine if packages are lost in transmission.
	Slower than UDP because error-checking each package requires more "work." Also, the loss of a package requires a request to resend the package, which can have an impact on subsequent packages.
	More reliable than UDP because all packages are verified.
	Example use: downloading of a software program.
ICMP	Internet Control Message Protocol.
	Support protocol for network devices.
	Used to send error messages and for determining the status of network devices.
	Unlike TCP or UDP in that it is designed to send simple messages, not transfer data between devices or establish connections between devices.
	Example use: **traceroute** and **ping**.

Knowledge of the Major Differences Between IPv4 and IPv6

The following table briefly describes the major differences between IPv4 and IPv6:

Difference	Description
Address scheme	IPv4: Dotted decimal notation, 32-bit number divided into four octets. IPv6: Hexadecimal notation, 128-bit number.
Number of available hosts	IPv4: Approximately 4.2 billion (with no extra subnetting). IPv6: A lot more than IPv4 (approximately 340,000,000,00 0,000,000,000,000,000,000,000,000,000).
Routing	IPv6 has a more efficient routing technique.
Autoconfiguration	IPv6 can be configured to auto-assign an IP address, much like DHCP in IPv4, but without needing a DHCP server.
Packet header	Each network package has a header that contains information about the packet. The header in IPv6 is much more complex and flexible.
Security	IPv4 relies on other protocols to provide security of the network packets whereas IPv6 has built-in security features.

Knowledge of the Basic Features of IPv6

See the "Knowledge of the Major Differences Between IPv4 and IPv6" section in this chapter.

/etc/services

The **/etc/services** file is the traditional location where services are mapped to ports. It is considered traditional in the sense that, historically, services would look to this file to determine which port they should use. However, most modern services have a setting in their configuration file that is used to determine the specific port they will use.

The **/etc/services** file is still useful to administrators in that it contains ports that have been assigned to services by the Internet Assigned Numbers Authority (IANA).

Each line in this file describes one service-to-port mapping. Here's the format of the line:

```
service_name    port/protocol    [alias]
```

For example:

```
[root@localhost ~]# grep smtp /etc/services
smtp            25/tcp          mail
smtp            25/udp          mail
urd             465/tcp             smtps    # URL Rendesvous Directory
for SSM / SMTP over SSL (TLS)
rsmtp           2390/tcp            # RSMTP
rsmtp           2390/udp            # RSMTP
```

IPv4, IPv6

See the "Knowledge of the Major Differences Between IPv4 and IPv6" section in this chapter.

Subnetting

See the "Demonstrate an Understanding of Network Masks and CIDR Notation" section in this chapter.

TCP, UDP, ICMP

See the "Knowledge About the Differences and Major Features of UDP, TCP, and ICMP" section in this chapter.

## CHAPTER 38

Basic Network Configuration

This chapter provides information and commands concerning the following topics:

- Manually and automatically configure network interfaces
- Basic TCP/IP host configuration
- Setting a default route
- **/etc/hostname**
- **/etc/hosts**
- **/etc/nsswitch.conf**
- **ifconfig**
- **ifup**
- **ifdown**
- **ip**
- **route**
- **ping**

Manually and Automatically Configure Network Interfaces

See the "ifconfig," "ifup," and "ifdown" sections in this chapter.

Basic TCP/IP Host Configuration

See the "/etc/hosts" and "/etc/nsswitch.conf" sections in this chapter.

Setting a Default Route

See the "route" section in this chapter.

/etc/hostname

The **/etc/hostname** file is where the local system's hostname is stored:

```
[root@localhost ~]# more /etc/hostname
server.sample999.com
```

/etc/hosts

The **/etc/hosts** file is where hostname-to-IP-address translation is defined:

```
[root@localhost ~]# more /etc/hosts
192.168.1.24 server.sample999.com
127.0.0.1    localhost localhost.localdomain localhost4 localhost4.
localdomain4
::1          localhost localhost.localdomain localhost6 localhost6.
localdomain6
```

Each line describes one translation. The first field is the IP address, the second field is the hostname, and the optional third field shows the alias addresses.

In most cases this file is only used for the local host itself or hosts on the local network. Normally hostname-to-IP-address translation is handled by a DNS server.

/etc/nsswitch.conf

The Name Service Switch (NSS) configuration file, **/etc/nsswitch.conf**, is used by applications to determine the sources from which to obtain name-service information, as well as in what order. For example, for networking, this file contains the location of the name server resolver, the utility that provides hostname-to-IP-address translation:

```
[root@localhost ~]# grep hosts /etc/nsswitch.conf
#hosts:     db files nisplus nis dns
hosts:      files dns
```

The value of **files dns** means "look at the local **/etc/hosts** file first, then look at the DNS server if the required translation isn't in the local file."

The following table describes common hostname-to-IP-address translation utilities:

Utility	Description
files	The local **/etc/hosts** file.
dns	A DNS server.
NIS	A Network Information Service server.

ifconfig

The **ifconfig** command displays basic IP network settings for devices:

```
[root@localhost ~]# ifconfig
enp0s3: flags=4163<UP,BROADCAST,RUNNING,MULTICAST>  mtu 1500
        inet 192.168.1.26 netmask 255.255.255.0  broadcast 192.168.1.255
        inet6 fe80::a00:27ff:feb0:dddc  prefixlen 64  scopeid 0x20<link>
        ether 08:00:27:b0:dd:dc  txqueuelen 1000  (Ethernet)
        RX packets 103224  bytes 17406939 (16.6 MiB)
```

```
RX errors 0   dropped 0   overruns 0   frame 0
TX packets 16408   bytes 3008229 (2.8 MiB)
TX errors 0   dropped 0 overruns 0   carrier 0   collisions 0

lo: flags=73<UP,LOOPBACK,RUNNING>   mtu 65536
        inet 127.0.0.1   netmask 255.0.0.0
        inet6 ::1   prefixlen 128   scopeid 0x10<host>
        loop   txqueuelen 0   (Local Loopback)
        RX packets 4891   bytes 257583 (251.5 KiB)
        RX errors 0   dropped 0   overruns 0   frame 0
        TX packets 4891   bytes 257583 (251.5 KiB)
        TX errors 0   dropped 0 overruns 0   carrier 0   collisions 0
```

The following table describes important options for the **ifconfig** command:

Option	Description
-a	Display all interfaces, even interfaces that are currently down.
-s	Display output like the **netstat -i** command.
-v	Verbose.

The **ifconfig** command can also be used to manually define network settings for a specific device. Here's an example:

```
ifconfig enp0s3 192.168.1.26   netmask 255.255.255.0 broadcast
192.168.1.255
```

NOTE: These changes are temporary and will only survive until the next time the system is booted. Permanent changes are made within your system's configuration files, which vary from one distribution to another.

Modern distributions will have the following message in the documentation for the **ifconfig** command:

"This program is obsolete! For replacement check ip addr and ip link. For statistics use ip -s link."

This is an accurate statement; however, if you are taking the LPIC exam, be aware that the **ifconfig** command is still testable on the exam.

ifup

The **ifup** command is designed to bring an interface up (for example, **ifup enp0s3**).

There are no critical options for this command.

ifdown

The **ifdown** command is designed to bring an interface up (for example, **ifdown enp0s3**). There are no critical options for this command.

ip

The **ip** command is a newer command that is designed to replace a collection of commands related to network interfaces. Here's the syntax for the **ip** command:

```
ip [options] object command
```

The following table describes some of the more important objects:

Object	Refers to
addr	IPv4 or IPv6 address.
link	Network device.
route	Routing table entry.

The following table describes the commands that can be executed:

Command	Description
add	Add an object.
delete	Delete an object.
show (or list)	Display information about an object.

The following example displays network information for devices, much like the **ifconfig** command:

```
[root@localhost ~]# ip addr show
1: lo: <LOOPBACK,UP,LOWER_UP> mtu 65536 qdisc noqueue state UNKNOWN
    link/loopback 00:00:00:00:00:00 brd 00:00:00:00:00:00
    inet 127.0.0.1/8 scope host lo
       valid_lft forever preferred_lft forever
    inet6 ::1/128 scope host
       valid_lft forever preferred_lft forever
2: enp0s3: <BROADCAST,MULTICAST,UP,LOWER_UP> mtu 1500 qdisc pfifo_fast
state UP qlen 1000
    link/ether 08:00:27:b0:dd:dc brd ff:ff:ff:ff:ff:ff
    inet 192.168.1.26/24 brd 192.168.1.255 scope global dynamic enp0s3
       valid_lft 2384sec preferred_lft 2384sec
    inet 192.168.1.24/16 brd 192.168.255.255 scope global enp0s3
       valid_lft forever preferred_lft forever
    inet6 fe80::a00:27ff:feb0:dddc/64 scope link
       valid_lft forever preferred_lft forever
```

route

The **route** command can be used to display the routing table:

```
[root@localhost ~]# route
Kernel IP routing table
Destination   Gateway       Genmask        Flags Metric Ref Use Iface
default       192.168.1.1   0.0.0.0        UG    100    0   0   enp0s3
192.168.0.0   0.0.0.0       255.255.0.0    U     100    0   0   enp0s3
192.168.1.0   0.0.0.0       255.255.255.0  U     100    0   0   enp0s3
```

This information can also be displayed with the **ip** command:

```
[root@localhost ~]# ip route show
default via 192.168.1.1 dev enp0s3  proto static   metric 100
192.168.0.0/16   dev enp0s3  proto kernel  scope link   src 192.168.1.24
metric 100
192.168.1.0/24   dev enp0s3  proto kernel  scope link   src 192.168.1.26
metric 100
192.168.122.0/24 dev virbr0  proto kernel  scope link   src 192.168.122.1
```

The **route** command can also be used to modify the default router:

```
route add default gw 192.168.1.10
```

To add a new router, execute the following command:

```
route add -net 192.168.3.0 netmask 255.255.255.0 gw 192.168.3.100
```

This command will send all network packets destined for the 192.168.3.0/24 network to the 192.168.3.100 router.

NOTE: These changes are temporary and will only survive until the next time the system is booted. Permanent changes are made within your system's configuration files, which vary from one distribution to another.

ping

The **ping** command is used to verify that a remote host can respond to a network connection:

```
[root@localhost ~]# ping -c 4 google.com
PING google.com (172.217.5.206) 56(84) bytes of data.
64 bytes from lax28s10-in-f14.1e100.net (172.217.5.206): icmp_seq=1
ttl=55 time=49.0 ms
64 bytes from lax28s10-in-f206.1e100.net (172.217.5.206): icmp_seq=2
ttl=55 time=30.2 ms
64 bytes from lax28s10-in-f14.1e100.net (172.217.5.206): icmp_seq=3
ttl=55 time=30.0 ms
64 bytes from lax28s10-in-f206.1e100.net (172.217.5.206): icmp_seq=4
ttl=55 time=29.5 ms
```

```
--- google.com ping statistics ---
4 packets transmitted, 4 received, 0% packet loss, time 3008ms
rtt min/avg/max/mdev = 29.595/34.726/49.027/8.261 ms
```

By default, the **ping** command will continuously send "pings" to the remote system until the user cancels the command (Ctrl+C). The **-c** option specifies a count of how many ping requests to send.

## CHAPTER 39

Basic Network Troubleshooting

This chapter provides information and commands concerning the following topics:

- Manually and automatically configure network interfaces and routing tables to include adding, starting, stopping, restarting, deleting, or reconfiguring network interfaces

- Change, view, or configure the routing table and correct an improperly set default route manually

- **ifconfig**

- **ip**

- **ifup**

- **ifdown**

- **route**

- **host**

- **hostname**

- **dig**

- **netstat**

- **ping**

- **ping6**

- **traceroute**

- **traceroute6**

- **tracepath**

- **tracepath6**

- **netcat**

Manually and Automatically Configure Network Interfaces and Routing Tables to Include Adding, Starting, Stopping, Restarting, Deleting, or Reconfiguring Network Interfaces

See the "ifconfig," "ip," "ifup," "ifdown," and "route" sections in Chapter 38, "Basic Network Configuration."

Change, View, or Configure the Routing Table and Correct an Improperly Set Default Route Manually

See the "route" section in Chapter 38.

ifconfig

See the "ifconfig" section in Chapter 38.

ip

See the "ip" section in Chapter 38.

ifup

See the "ifup" section in Chapter 38.

ifdown

See the "ifdown" section in Chapter 38.

route

See the "route" section in Chapter 38.

host

The **host** command is normally used to perform simple hostname-to-IP-address translation operations (also called *DNS queries*):

```
[root@localhost ~]# host google.com
google.com has address 172.217.4.142
google.com has IPv6 address 2607:f8b0:4007:800::200e
google.com mail is handled by 30 alt2.aspmx.l.google.com.
google.com mail is handled by 50 alt4.aspmx.l.google.com.
google.com mail is handled by 20 alt1.aspmx.l.google.com.
google.com mail is handled by 10 aspmx.l.google.com.
google.com mail is handled by 40 alt3.aspmx.l.google.com.
```

The following table describes common options for the **dig** command:

Option	Description
-t	Specify a type of query that you want to display; for example, **host -t ns google.com** will display Google's name servers.
-4	Only perform IPv4 queries.
-6	Only perform IPv6 queries.
-v	Verbose; output is like that of the **dig** command.

hostname

The **hostname** command can display or change the system hostname:

```
[root@localhost ~]# hostname
server.sample999.com
[root@localhost ~]# hostname myhost
[root@server ~]# hostname
myhost
```

dig

The **dig** command is useful for performing DNS queries on specific DNS servers. The format of the command is demonstrated here:

```
[root@localhost ~]# dig google.com


; <<>> DiG 9.9.4-RedHat-9.9.4-38.el7_3 <<>> google.com
;; global options: +cmd
;; Got answer:
;; ->>HEADER<<- opcode: QUERY, status: NOERROR, id: 56840
;; flags: qr rd ra; QUERY: 1, ANSWER: 1, AUTHORITY: 0, ADDITIONAL: 1

;; OPT PSEUDOSECTION:
; EDNS: version: 0, flags:; udp: 512
;; QUESTION SECTION:
;google.com.                    IN      A

;; ANSWER SECTION:
google.com.             268     IN      A       216.58.217.206

;; Query time: 36 msec
;; SERVER: 192.168.1.1#53(192.168.1.1)
;; WHEN: Sun Mar 05 17:01:08 PST 2017
;; MSG SIZE  rcvd: 55
```

To query a specific DNS server, rather than the default DNS servers for your host, use the following syntax: **dig @server host_to_lookup**.

The following table describes common options for the **dig** command:

Option	Description
-f *file*	Use the content of *file* to perform multiple lookups; the file should contain one hostname per line.
-4	Only perform IPv4 queries.
-6	Only perform IPv6 queries.
-x address	Perform a reverse lookup (return the hostname when provided an IP address).

netstat

The **netstat** command is useful for displaying a variety of network information. It is a key utility when troubleshooting network issues. The following table describes common options for the **netstat** command:

Option	Description
-t or **--tcp**	Display TCP information.
-u or **--udp**	Display UDP information.
-r or **--route**	Display the routing table.
-v or **--verbose**	Verbose; display additional information.
-i or **--interfaces**	Display information based on a specific interface.
-a or **--all**	Apply to all.
-s or **--statistics**	Display statistics for the output.

For example, the following command will display all active TCP connections:

```
[root@localhost ~]# netstat -ta
Active Internet connections (servers and established)
Proto Recv-Q Send-Q Local Address        Foreign Address
State
tcp        0      0 192.168.122.1:domain  0.0.0.0:*
LISTEN
tcp        0      0 0.0.0.0:ssh           0.0.0.0:*
LISTEN
tcp        0      0 localhost:ipp         0.0.0.0:*
LISTEN
tcp        0      0 localhost:smtp        0.0.0.0:*
LISTEN
tcp6       0      0 [::]:ssh              [::]:*
LISTEN
tcp6       0      0 localhost:ipp         [::]:*
LISTEN
tcp6       0      0 localhost:smtp        [::]:*
LISTEN
```

ping

See the "ping" section in Chapter 38.

ping6

The **ping6** command is similar to the **ping** command, except it is used to ping IPv6 addresses, whereas the **ping** command is used to ping IPv4 addresses. See the "ping" section in Chapter 38.

traceroute

The **traceroute** command is used to display the router hops from one system to another:

```
[root@localhost ~]# traceroute google.com
traceroute to google.com (172.217.4.142), 30 hops max, 60 byte packets
 1  * * *
 2  * * *
 3  * * *
 4  * * *
 5  * * *
 6  * paltbprj02-ae1-308.rd.pt.cox.net (68.105.31.37)   49.338 ms
53.183 ms
 7  108.170.242.83 (108.170.242.83)   53.041 ms 108.170.242.82
(108.170.242.82)   57.529 ms 108.170.242.227 (108.170.242.227)   60.106
ms
 8  209.85.246.38 (209.85.246.38)   56.051 ms 209.85.246.20
(209.85.246.20)   59.853 ms 209.85.249.63 (209.85.249.63)   64.812 ms
 9  64.233.174.204 (64.233.174.204)   59.018 ms 64.233.174.206
(64.233.174.206)   59.307 ms 64.233.174.204 (64.233.174.204)   57.352 ms
10  64.233.174.191 (64.233.174.191)   67.186 ms   66.823 ms 209.85.247.0
(209.85.247.0)   65.519 ms
11  108.170.247.193 (108.170.247.193)   65.097 ms 108.170.247.225
(108.170.247.225)   65.039 ms 108.170.247.193 (108.170.247.193)   38.324
ms
12  72.14.238.213 (72.14.238.213)   41.229 ms   40.340 ms   41.887 ms
13  lax17s14-in-f142.1e100.net (172.217.4.142)   43.281 ms   40.650 ms
43.394 ms
```

NOTE: The value of * means that the data for that hop could not be retrieved.

The following table describes common options for the **traceroute** command:

Option	Description
-n	Only display IP addresses; don't resolve to hostnames.
-6	Perform an IPv6 traceroute (IPv4 is used by default).
-g or **--gateway**	Specify the router (gateway) to perform the traceroute through.
-i or **--interface**	Specify the interface (network device) to perform the traceroute through.

traceroute6

The **traceroute6** command is the same as the **traceroute** command when the **-6** option is used. See the "traceroute" section in this chapter for more details.

tracepath

The **tracepath** command is similar to the **traceroute** command, with two notable exceptions:

- The **traceroute** command can only be executed by the root user, whereas any user can use the **tracepath** command.

- The **tracepath** command lacks many of the options that the **traceroute** command provides. For example, it supports the **-n** option (display IP addresses, not hostnames) but not the **-i** and **-g** options that the **traceroute** command supports.

See the "traceroute" section in this chapter for more details.

tracepath6

The **tracepath6** command is just like the **tracepath** command, but for IPv6 queries. See the "tracepath" section in this chapter for more details.

netcat

The **netcat** command (just **nc** or **ncat** on many distributions) is a utility that can be used for debugging network issues. For example, you can have the **nc** command act as a server that is listening on a specific port:

```
[root@localhost ~]# nc -l 9000
```

You can also use the **nc** command to connect to a server on a specific port:

```
[root@localhost ~]# nc localhost 9000
```

Now whatever messages you send on the client side show up on the server side, and vice versa. This utility allows you to test interactions with existing servers as well as allows you to create your own simple network server.

The following table describes common options for the **nc** command:

Option	Description
-4	Allow only IPv4 communication.
-6	Allow only IPv6 communication.
-l or **--listen**	Open a port to listen on.
-k or **--keep-open**	Don't close the server port when client disconnects; keep the server alive for additional connections.
-m or **--max-conns**	Establish the maximum number of connections allowed to the server.

## CHAPTER 40

Configure Client-Side DNS

This chapter provides information and commands concerning the following topics:

- Query remote DNS servers
- Configure local name resolution and use remote DNS servers
- Modify the order in which name resolution is done
- **/etc/hosts**
- **/etc/resolv.conf**
- **/etc/nsswitch.conf**
- **host**
- **dig**
- **getent**

Query Remote DNS Servers

See the "host" and "dig" sections in Chapter 39, "Basic Network Troubleshooting."

Configure local name resolution and use remote DNS servers

See the "/etc/resolv.conf" section in this chapter.

Modify the Order in Which Name Resolution Is Done

See the "/etc/nsswitch.conf" section in Chapter 38, "Basic Network Configuration."

/etc/hosts

See the "/etc/hosts" section in Chapter 38.

/etc/resolv.conf

The **/etc/resolv.conf** file contains a list of the DNS servers for the system. A typical file looks like the following:

```
[root@localhost ~]# cat /etc/resolv.conf
```

```
search sample999.com
nameserver 192.168.1
```

If you are using a utility such as NetworkManager to configure your network settings or are using a DHCP client, then this file is normally populated by those utilities. For servers, this file is typically manually defined.

The following table describes common settings for the **/etc/resolv.conf** file:

Setting	Description
nameserver	The IP address of the DNS server; there can be up to three **nameserver** lines in the file.
domain	Used to specify the local domain, which allows for use of short names for DNS queries.
search	A list of optional domains to perform DNS queries on when using short names.

/etc/nsswitch.conf

See the "/etc/nsswitch.conf" section in Chapter 38.

host

See the "host" section in Chapter 39.

dig

See the "dig" section in Chapter 39.

getent

The getent command can perform queries on database entries, such as hostname queries. See the "getent" section in Chapter 30, "Manage User and Group Accounts and Related System Files," for more details regarding this command.

## CHAPTER 41

Perform Security Administration Tasks

This chapter provides information and commands concerning the following topics:

- Audit a system to find files with the suid/sgid bit set
- Set or change user passwords and password-aging information
- Being able to use nmap and netstat to discover open ports on a system
- Set up limits on user logins, processes, and memory usage
- Determine which users have logged in to the system or are currently logged in
- Basic sudo configuration and usage
- **find**
- **passwd**
- **fuser**
- **lsof**
- **nmap**
- **chage**
- **netstat**
- **sudo**
- **/etc/sudoers**
- **su**
- **usermod**
- **ulimit**
- **who, w, last**

Audit a System to Find Files with the suid/sgid Bit Set

The following command can be used to search for files with the suid (also called setuid) bit set:

```
find / -perm -4000 -ls
```

The following command can be used to search for files with the sgid (also called setgid) bit set:

```
find / -perm -2000 -ls
```

See the "find" section in Chapter 23, "Find System Files and Place Files in the Correct Location," for further details regarding the **find** command.

Set or Change User Passwords and Password-Aging Information

See the "passwd" and "chage" sections in Chapter 30, "Manage User and Group Accounts and Related System Files," for details.

Being Able to Use nmap and netstat to Discover Open Ports on a System

See the "nmap" section in this chapter and the "netstat" section in Chapter 39, "Basic Network Troubleshooting," for details.

Set Up Limits on User Logins, Processes, and Memory Usage

See the "ulimit" section in this chapter for details.

Determine Which Users Have Logged in to the System or Are Currently Logged In

See the "who, w, last" section in this chapter for details.

Basic sudo Configuration and Usage

See the "sudo" and "/etc/sudoers" sections in this chapter for details.

find

See the "find" section in Chapter 23 for details.

passwd

See the "passwd" section in Chapter 30 for details.

fuser

The **fuser** command is useful to determine which files are using system resources. One of the more common uses of this command is to determine which user is active in a filesystem, which prevents the system administrator from unmounting the filesystem:

```
[root@localhost ~]# umount /boot
umount: /boot: target is busy.
        (In some cases useful info about processes that use
        the device is found by lsof(8) or fuser(1))
[root@localhost ~]# fuser -v /boot
```

```
                USER        PID ACCESS   COMMAND
/boot:          root        kernel       mount /boot
                student     29306        ..c.. bash
```

The ACCESS column can contain useful information as to how the user is using the file-system:

Character	Description
c	Filesystem is being used as the current directory of the process.
e	An executable process is being run from the filesystem.
f	A file is open from the filesystem.
F	A file is open for writing from the filesystem.
r	Filesystem is being used as the root directory for the user's virtual filesystem.

The following table describes common options for the **fuser** command:

Option	Description
-k or **--kill**	Kill the process that is using the filesystem or resource.
-i or **--interactive**	Prompt before killing the process (you must also use the **-k** option).
-v or **--verbose**	Verbose; produce additional useful information.

lsof

The **lsof** command is used to list open files. When used with no arguments, it will list all of the open files for the OS:

```
[root@localhost ~]# lsof | wc -l
25466
```

A more useful technique would be to list all files related to open network connections:

```
[root@localhost ~]# lsof -i
COMMAND     PID   USER    FD  TYPE  DEVICE  SIZE/OFF  NODE  NAME
avahi-dae   674   avahi   13u IPv4  15730   0t0       UDP   *:mdns
avahi-dae   674   avahi   14u IPv4  15731   0t0       UDP   *:49932
sshd        1411  root    3u  IPv4  18771   0t0       TCP   *:ssh (LISTEN)
sshd        1411  root    4u  IPv6  18779   0t0       TCP   *:ssh (LISTEN)
master      2632  root    14u IPv4  20790   0t0       TCP   localhost:smtp
(LISTEN)
master      2632  root    15u IPv6  20791   0t0       TCP   localhost:smtp
(LISTEN)
dnsmasq     2739  nobody  3u  IPv4  21518   0t0       UDP   *:bootps
dnsmasq     2739  nobody  5u  IPv4  21525   0t0       UDP
```

```
192.168.122.1:domain

dnsmasq    2739     nobody   6u   IPv4    21526      0t0   TCP
192.168.122.1:domain (LISTEN)

cupsd      4099     root    12u   IPv6    564510     0t0   TCP
localhost:ipp (LISTEN)

cupsd      4099     root    13u   IPv4    564511     0t0   TCP
localhost:ipp (LISTEN)

dhclient   26133    root     6u   IPv4    1151444    0t0   UDP  *:bootpc

dhclient   26133    root    20u   IPv4    1151433    0t0   UDP  *:14638

dhclient   26133    root    21u   IPv6    1151434    0t0   UDP  *:47997
```

The following table describes common options for the **lsof** command:

Option	Description
-i	Match the Internet address; could also be used to display based on IP version (**-i4** or **-i6**) or port (**-i TCP:80**), or to display all open connections.
-u *user*	List files opened by *user*.
-p *pid*	List files opened by the process with a process ID of *pid*.

nmap

The **nmap** command is used to probe a system for open network ports. Typically this is run against a remote system, but for testing purposes, the local system can be used:

```
[student@localhost ~]# nmap localhost

Starting Nmap 6.40 ( http://nmap.org ) at 2017-03-06 21:38 PST
Nmap scan report for localhost (127.0.0.1)
Host is up (0.0000060s latency).
Other addresses for localhost (not scanned): 127.0.0.1
Not shown: 997 closed ports
PORT     STATE SERVICE
22/tcp   open  ssh
25/tcp   open  smtp
631/tcp  open  ipp

Nmap done: 1 IP address (1 host up) scanned in 0.05 seconds
```

The following table describes common options for the **lsof** command:

Option	Description
-sn	Scan an entire network to determine what machines are active.
-p	Specify which ports to scan (for example, **nmap p 1-1024**).
-sV	Probe the port to determine the software and its version.

Option	Description
-sS	Perform a SYN scan, which tends to be a quicker scanning method.
-v	Enable verbose mode.
-A	Will also attempt to determine the operating system (OS) and its version.
-T4	Used to speed up the execution of the **nmap** utility.

chage

See the "chage" section in Chapter 30 for details.

netstat

See the "netstat" section in Chapter 39 for details.

sudo

When properly configured by the administrator, users can use the **sudo** command to run commands as other users (typically as the root user). To execute a command as root, enter the following:

```
sudo command
```

You will be prompted for your own password and, if the settings in the **/etc/sudoers** file are correct, the command will execute correctly. If the settings are not correct, an error message will appear.

The following table describes common options for the **lsof** command:

Option	Description
-b	Run the command in the background.
-l	List which commands are allowed for this user.
-u *user*	Run command as *user* rather than as the root user.

Also see the "/etc/sudoers" section in this chapter.

/etc/sudoers

The **/etc/sudoers** file is used to determine which users can use the **sudo** command to execute commands as other users (typically as the root user). To edit this file, you must be logged in as the root user and should use the **visudo** command rather than edit the file directly.

The following table describes important definitions for the **/etc/sudoers** file:

Option	Description
User_Alias	A name that represents a group of users (for example, **User_Alias ADMINS = julia, sarah**)
Cmnd_Alias	A name that represents a group of commands (for example, **Cmnd_Alias SOFTWARE = /bin/rpm, /usr/bin/yum**).

The format of an entry for the **/etc/sudoers** file uses the following syntax:

```
user          machine=commands
```

To allow the student user the ability to execute the **/usr/bin/yum** command as the root user, add an entry like the following to the **/etc/sudoers** file:

```
student          ALL=/usr/bin/yum
```

To allow all members of ADMINS the ability to execute all of the **SOFTWARE** command as the root user, add an entry like the following to the **/etc/sudoers** file:

```
ADMINS    ALL=SOFTWARE
```

su

The **su** command allows a user to shift user accounts:

```
[student@localhost ~]# id
uid=1000(student) gid=1000(student) groups=1000(student)
context=unconfined_u:unconfined_r:unconfined_t:s0-s0:c0.c1023
[student@localhost ~]# su root
Password:
[root@localhost ~]# id
uid=0(root) gid=0(root) groups=0(root)
context=unconfined_u:unconfined_r:unconfined_t:s0-s0:c0.c1023
```

One option is permitted when executing the **su** command: the - option. When you execute the **su** command with the - option, a new login shell will be provided. When not using the - character, a non-login shell will be provided.

usermod

The **usermod** command allows an administrator to change a user account. See the "usermod" section in Chapter 31, "Automate System Administration Tasks by Scheduling Jobs," for more details.

ulimit

The **ulimit** command lists or sets a user's account limits:

```
[root@localhost ~]# ulimit -a
core file size          (blocks, -c) 0
data seg size           (kbytes, -d) unlimited
scheduling priority             (-e) 0
file size               (blocks, -f) unlimited
pending signals                 (-i) 15439
max locked memory       (kbytes, -l) 64
max memory size         (kbytes, -m) unlimited
open files                      (-n) 1024
pipe size            (512 bytes, -p) 8
POSIX message queues     (bytes, -q) 819200
real-time priority              (-r) 0
stack size              (kbytes, -s) 8192
cpu time               (seconds, -t) unlimited
max user processes              (-u) 4096
virtual memory          (kbytes, -v) unlimited
file locks                      (-x) unlimited
```

These limits are normally configured by the system administrator using a PAM configuration file:

```
[root@localhost ~]# tail -n 12 /etc/security/limits.conf
#<domain>        <type>  <item>          <value>
#

#*               soft    core            0
#*               hard    rss             10000
#@student        hard    nproc           20
#@faculty        soft    nproc           20
#@faculty        hard    nproc           50
#ftp             hard    nproc           0
#@student        -       maxlogins       4

# End of file
```

For example, you may want to limit how many concurrent logins an account can have:

```
student         -       maxlogins       4
```

Users rarely use the **ulimit** command to limit their own account, so the options for this command are not as important as understanding what the output displays. Additionally, some of the limits are very rarely used. The commonly used limits are described in the following table:

Limit	Description
fsize	Maximum file size allowed in memory.
cpu	Maximum CPU time allowed.
nproc	Maximum number of concurrently running processes.
maxlogins	Maximum number of concurrent logins.

who, w, last

The **who** command shows who is currently logged in:

```
[root@localhost ~]# who
student   :0            2017-02-18 01:52 (:0)
student   pts/0         2017-02-18 01:52 (:0)
student   pts/1         2017-03-05 19:55 (:0)
student   pts/2         2017-03-06 18:24 (:0)
root      pts/3         2017-03-06 18:24 (localhost)
```

The output of the **who** command includes the username, the terminal device the user is using, the login date and time and where the user logged in from (**:0** means a local login). The following table describes common options for the **who** command:

Option	Description
-b or --boot	Time of the last system boot.
-H or --heading	Display headings on columns.
-q or --count	Display the number of users currently logged in.

The **w** command displays who is logged in as well as other useful information:

```
[root@localhost ~]# w
 18:25:08 up 3 days,  1:24,  5 users,  load average: 0.27, 0.08, 0.07
USER     TTY      FROM        LOGIN@   IDLE   JCPU   PCPU  WHAT
student  :0       :0          18Feb17  ?xdm?  41:48  1.01s gdm-session-wor
student  pts/0    :0          18Feb17  4.00s  0.46s 20.33s /usr/libexec/gn
student  pts/1    :0          Sun19    1:32   0.04s  0.00s less -s
student  pts/2    :0          18:24    12.00s 0.05s  0.01s /usr/bin/sss_ss
root     pts/3    localhost   18:24    12.00s 0.03s  0.03s -bash
```

The first line of output is the same as the **uptime** command. See the "uptime" section in Chapter 13, "Create, Monitor, and Kill Processes," for more details. The JCPU column stands for "Job CPU" and represents how much CPU time has been used by all processes that were launched from the terminal. The PCPU column stands for "Process CPU" and represents how much CPU time has been used by the current process (which is listed as the last item in the line of output).

The following table describes common options for the **w** command:

Option	Description
-h or **--no-header**	Don't display headings on columns.
-s or **--short**	Short; don't display JCPU or PCPU columns.

The **last** command displays information about current and previous logins:

```
[root@localhost ~]# last -10
root      pts/3           localhost     Mon Mar  6 18:24    still logged in
student   pts/2           :0            Mon Mar  6 18:24    still logged in
student   pts/1           :0            Sun Mar  5 19:55    still logged in
student   pts/1    :0     Sat Feb 18 01:56 - 01:56  (00:00)
student   pts/0    :0     Sat Feb 18 01:52    still logged in
student   :0       :0     Sat Feb 18 01:52    still logged in
(unknown  :0       :0     Sat Feb 18 01:48 - 01:52  (00:03)
reboot    system boot  3.10.0-327.18.2. Tue Jan 24 13:43 - 19:15
(41+05:31)
student   pts/1    :0     Sun Jan 22 08:22 - 01:46 (26+17:24)
student   pts/0    :0     Thu Jan 19 12:19 - 01:46 (29+13:27)

wtmp begins Sat Jun 11 20:51:56 2016
```

The following table describes common options for the **last** command:

Option	Description
-x	Only show x number of logins.
-a	Display the hostname for remote logins.
-d	Display the IP address for logins.
-F	Display the full login and logout times.

## CHAPTER 42

Set Up Host Security

This chapter provides information and commands concerning the following topics:

- Awareness of shadow passwords and how they work
- Turn off network services not in use
- Understand the role of TCP Wrappers
- **/etc/nologin**
- **/etc/passwd**
- **/etc/shadow**
- **/etc/xinetd.d/**
- **/etc/xinetd.conf**
- **/etc/inetd.d/**
- **/etc/inetd.conf**
- **/etc/inittab**
- **/etc/init.d/**
- **/etc/hosts.allow**
- **/etc/hosts.deny**

Awareness of Shadow Passwords and How They Work

See the "/etc/shadow" section in Chapter 30, "Manage User and Group Accounts and Related System Files," for details.

Turn Off Network Services Not in Use

There is more than one method for turning off network services that are not in use:

- If the service is a standalone service, such as an SSH server, then stop the process that provides the service. How this can be accomplished depends on your distribution. See the "init" and "systemd" sections in Chapter 3, "Change Runlevels / Boot Targets and Shutdown or Reboot System."

- If the service is started by another process, such as the **inetd** or **xinetd** daemon, use the configuration files for that daemon to turn off the network service. See the "/etc/xinetd.d/," "/etc/xinetd.conf," "/etc/inetd.d/," and "/etc/inetd.conf" sections in this chapter for details.

Understand the Role of TCP Wrappers

One of the techniques to filter access to services on a host is a library called TCP Wrappers. This library uses simple configuration files (the **/etc/hosts.allow** and **/etc/ hosts.deny** files) to either allow or deny access from specific hosts or networks.

Only services that use the TCP Wrappers library will be affected by the **/etc/hosts.allow** and **/etc/hosts.deny** files. You can determine if a program uses this library by using the **ldd** command:

```
[root@localhost ~]# which sshd
/usr/sbin/sshd
[root@localhost ~]# ldd /usr/sbin/sshd | grep libwrap
        libwrap.so.0 => /lib64/libwrap.so.0 (0x00002b003df03000)
```

TCP Wrappers uses the following steps to determine whether access should be allowed or denied:

1. If a match is made in the **/etc/hosts.allow** file, then access is granted. If not, then the next step is consulted.

2. If a match is made in the **/etc/hosts.deny** file, then access is denied. If not, then the next step is consulted.

3. If no matches are made in either file, then access is granted.

The format of the **/etc/hosts.allow** and **/etc/hosts.deny** file is as follows:

```
service:        hosts|network
```

The following explicitly allows access to the SSHD server for the 192.168.1.1 hosts and the 192.168.99.0/24 network:

```
[root@localhost ~]# cat /etc/hosts.allow
sshd: 192.168.1.1
sshd: 192.168.99.0/24
```

The following table describes how the service can be specified:

Item	Description
service	Matches a single service.
service,service	Matches any of the services listed. (Note that there's no space between services.)
ALL	Matches all services.

The following table describes how the host or network can be specified:

Item	Description
IP	An IP address.
Hostname	A hostname that can be resolved.

Item	Description
@*group*	A NIS group.
Network	Any of these formats are permitted: 192.168.1., 192.168.99.0/24, 192.168.99.0/255.255.255.0, or .example.com.

/etc/nologin

If this file exists, regular users are not permitted to log in to the system. If this file contains text data, the contents of this file are displayed to the user if a login attempt is made.

/etc/passwd

See the "/etc/passwd" section in Chapter 30 for details.

/etc/shadow

See the "/etc/shadow" section in Chapter 30 for details.

/etc/xinetd.d/

The files in the **/etc/xinetd.d** directory are used to override and supplement settings from the **/etc/xinetd.conf** file. The following example is for the Telnet service:

```
[root@localhost ~]# cat /etc/xinetd.d/telnet
# default: on
# description: The telnet server serves telnet sessions; it uses \
#       unencrypted username/password pairs for authentication.
service telnet
{
        flags          = REUSE
        socket_type    = stream
        wait           = no
        user           = root
        server         = /usr/sbin/in.telnetd
        log_on_failure += USERID
        disable        = yes
}
```

The following table describes common settings of files in the **/etc/xinetd.d** directory:

Setting	Description
user	Which user to run the service as.
server	The executable file for the service.

Setting	Description
log_on_failure	What data to store in the log entry if a failed login attempt occurs.
disable	When **disable** is set to **yes**, the service is not enabled; when it's set to **no**, the service is enabled.

/etc/xinetd.conf

The **xinetd** daemon is referred to as the "super daemon" because it will start other daemons as needed and stop them when they are no longer needed. The primary configuration file for the **xinetd** daemon is the **/etc/xinetd.conf** file.

The following table describes common settings in the **/etc/xinetd.conf** file:

Setting	Description
cps	Used to limit how many connection attempts are made to avoid a denial-of-service attack. Two arguments are given (for example, **cpu 50 10**). The first value is how many connections per second are permitted. The second value is how long to disable the service if the connections per section are exceeded (10 seconds in this example).
instances	How many concurrent connections are allowed.
per_source	How many concurrent connections from a specific host are allowed.
includedir	The directory where additional rules can be included. See the "/etc/xinetd.d/" section in this chapter for more information.

/etc/inetd.d/

The files in the **/etc/inetd.d** directory are used to configure specific services controlled by the **inetd** daemon. See the "/etc/inetd.conf" section in this chapter for more details.

/etc/inetd.conf

The **inetd** daemon is referred to as the "super daemon" because it will start other daemons as needed and stop them when they are no longer needed. The primary configuration file for the **inetd** daemon is the **/etc/inetd.conf** file.

> **IMPORTANT NOTE:** The **inetd** daemon has been replace by the **xinetd** daemon on modern Linus distributions; however, **inetd** is still a testable topic for the LPIC exams. For the exam, you should just be aware of what **inetd** is and what configuration files it uses.

/etc/inittab

See the "/etc/inittab" section in Chapter 3.

/etc/init.d/

See the "/etc/init.d" section in Chapter 3.

/etc/hosts.allow

See the "Understand the Role of TCP Wrappers" section in this chapter.

/etc/hosts.deny

See the "Understand the Role of TCP Wrappers" section in this chapter.

## CHAPTER 43

Securing Data with Encryption

This chapter provides information and commands concerning the following topics:

- Perform basic OpenSSH 2 client configuration and usage
- Understand the role of OpenSSH 2 server host keys
- Perform basic GnuPG configuration, usage, and revocation
- Understand SSH port tunnels (including X11 tunnels)
- **ssh**
- **ssh-keygen**
- **ssh-agent**
- **ssh-add**
- **~/.ssh/id_rsa and id_rsa.pub**
- **~/.ssh/id_dsa and id_dsa.pub**
- **/etc/ssh/ssh_host_rsa_key and ssh_host_rsa_key.pub**
- **/etc/ssh/ssh_host_dsa_key and ssh_host_dsa_key.pub**
- **~/.ssh/authorized_keys**
- **ssh_known_hosts**
- **gpg**
- **~/.gnupg/**

Perform Basic OpenSSH 2 Client Configuration and Usage

See the "ssh," "ssh-keygen," "ssh-agent," and "ssh-add" sections in this chapter.

Understand the Role of OpenSSH 2 Server Host Keys

See the "/etc/ssh/ssh_host_rsa_key and ssh_host_rsa_key.pub" and "/etc/ssh/ssh_host_dsa_key and ssh_host_dsa_key.pub" sections in this file.

Perform Basic GnuPG Configuration, Usage, and Revocation

See the "gpg" section in this chapter.

Understand SSH Port Tunnels (Including X11 Tunnels)

Many network protocols do not provide the means of encrypting the network traffic. A Secure Shell (SSH) port tunnel can be created to forward network packets between SSH servers, providing encryption of such data.

You can create two types of port tunnels:

- **Local**—Where data is sent to a local port and the SSH server sends the data to a remote port. For example, a local tunnel could be configured to forward all traffic sent to the local port 2222 to port 80 on a remote host. This is also called an *outgoing tunnel*.

- **Remote**—Where data is forwarded from a remote port to a local port. For example, incoming traffic destined for port 2222 on the server could be forwarded to port 80 on the local host. This is also called an *incoming tunnel*.

A local port tunnel is created by a command like the following:

```
ssh -L 8586:localhost:8586 user@server
```

A remote port tunnel is created by a command like the following:

```
ssh user@server -R 8000:192.168.1.12:8000
```

An X11 tunnel is one that forwards GUI application data across an SSH session. When the **-X** option is used to establish an SSH connection to a remote system, the X11 tunnel will automatically be configured:

```
ssh -X user@remote_host
```

This means that after logging in to the remote host, the user can execute a program that provides a GUI interface, and that interface will be displayed back on the local system.

ssh

The **ssh** command is a utility that allows you to connect to a Secure Shell (SSH) server. The syntax of the command is as follows:

```
ssh user@hostname
```

Replace *user* with the username that you want to use to log in as and replace *hostname* with a system hostname or IP address.

The first time you use the **ssh** command to connect to a system, it will issue the following prompt:

```
[root@localhost ~]# ssh bob@server1
The authenticity of host 'server1' can't be established.
ECDSA key fingerprint is 8a:d9:88:b0:e8:05:d6:2b:85:df:53:10:54:66:5f:0f.
Are you sure you want to continue connecting (yes/no)?
```

This is to ensure that you are logging in to the correct system. Typically users answer "yes" to this prompt, assuming they are logging in to the correct machine, but this information can also be verified independently by contacting the system administrator of the remote system.

After the user answers "yes" to this prompt, the SSH server fingerprint is stored in the **known_hosts** file in the **~/.ssh** directory.

The following table describes common options for the **ssh** command:

Option	Description
-F configfile	Specify the configuration file to use for the ssh client utility. The default configuration file is **/etc/ssh/ssh_config**. See the "Perform Basic OpenSSH 2 Client Configuration and Usage" section in this chapter for details regarding this file.
-4	Only use IPv4 addresses.
-6	Only use IPv6 addresses.
-E logfile	Place errors in the specified log file rather than displaying them to standard output.

ssh-keygen

The **ssh-keygen** command can be used to generate authentication keys. A common use for this command is to create the authentication files that are used for password-less authentication:

```
[julia@localhost ~]# ssh-keygen
Generating public/private rsa key pair.
Enter file in which to save the key (/home/julia/.ssh/id_rsa):
Enter passphrase (empty for no passphrase):
Enter same passphrase again:
Your identification has been saved in /home/julia/.ssh/id_rsa.
Your public key has been saved in /home/julia/.ssh/id_rsa.pub.
The key fingerprint is:
6d:40:24:e2:3e:62:7f:a4:f0:5d:d5:05:1b:06:fd:d7 bo@ubuntu
The key's randomart image is:

+--[ RSA 2048]----+
|    . ..o .o+..   |
|   . . o   o.+    |
|    .    . . o.  .|
|    .      +    . E|
|   + o . S o    . |
|  . = = . .      |
|    + o          |
|     .           |
|                 |
+-----------------+
```

The result of this command is two new files: **~/.ssh/id_rsa** and **~/.ssh.id_rsa.pub**. The content of these files is used for password authentication in conjunction with the **~/.ssh/ authorized_keys** file. See the "~/.ssh/authorized_keys" section in this chapter for details.

RSA is an encryption algorithm. Another popular encryption algorithm is DSA. To use DSA instead of RSA, use the **-t DSA** option to the **ssh-keygen** command. The result of using this option is two new files: **~/.ssh/id_dsa** and **~/.ssh.id_dsa.pub**.

> **NOTE:** If a passphrase is requested during the execution of the **ssh-keygen** command, this passphrase would need to be entered in place of a password whenever an SSH connection is established. Repeatedly entering this passphrase can be avoided by using the **ssh-agent** and **ssh-add** utilities. See the "ssh-agent" and "ssh-add" sections in this chapter for details regarding these utilities.

ssh-agent

The **ssh-agent** utility is used to avoid needing to enter a passphrase whenever password-less SSH authentication is used. See the "ssh-keygen" section in this chapter for details regarding setting up password-less SSH authentication.

One way to use this feature is to execute the following command: **ssh-agent bash**. A shell is started in which the SSH agent will cache added RSA and DSA encryption keys. These keys can be added to the SSH agent cache with the **ssh-add** command. See the "ssh-add" section in this chapter for more details.

ssh-add

After the **ssh-agent** utility has been started, the **ssh-add** command can be used to add RSA and DSA encryption keys to the SSH agent's cache. See the "ssh-agent" section in this chapter to learn how to start this utility.

To use the **ssh-add** utility, execute the command with no arguments:

```
[julia@localhost ~]# ssh-add
Identity added: /home/julia/.ssh/id_rsa (/home/julia/.ssh/id_rsa)
```

After the keys have been added, they are automatically used in future SSH connections.

~/.ssh/id_rsa and id_rsa.pub

The content of the **~/.ssh/id_rsa** and **id_rsa.pub** files is used for password authentication in conjunction with the **ssh-agent** and **ssh-add** utilities. See the "ssh-agent" and "ssh-add" sections in this chapter for details regarding these utilities.

~/.ssh/id_dsa and id_dsa.pub

The content of the **~/.ssh/id_dsa** and **id_dsa.pub** files is used for password authentication in conjunction with the **ssh-agent** and **ssh-add** utilities. See the "ssh-agent" and "ssh-add" sections in this chapter for details regarding these utilities.

/etc/ssh/ssh_host_rsa_key and ssh_host_rsa_key.pub

The **/etc/ssh/ssh_host_rsa_key** and **/etc/ssh/ssh_host_rsa_key.pub** files are used by the Secure Shell server to encrypt data that is transferred between the client and the server programs. Data is encrypted using the RSA encryption algorithm and the keys in these files. The RSA encryption method is used by default, but the DSA encryption method could also be used.

/etc/ssh/ssh_host_dsa_key and ssh_host_dsa_key.pub

The **/etc/ssh/ssh_host_dsa_key** and **/etc/ssh/ssh_host_dsa_key.pub** files are used by the Secure Shell server to encrypt data that is transferred between the client and the server programs.

The RSA encryption method is used by default, but the DSA encryption method could also be used. Data is encrypted using DSA encryption algorithm and the keys in these files.

~/.ssh/authorized_keys

When a user wants to use password-based SSH authentication, the first step is to create authentication keys by using the **ssh-keygen** command. See the "ssh-keygen" section for details regarding this process.

After the authentication key files have been created, the public key (the contents of either the **~/.ssh/id_dsa.pub** or **~/.ssh/id_rsa.pub** file) need to be copied to the system that the user is attempting to log in to. This requires placing the public key into the **~/.ssh/authorized_keys** file on the SSH server. This can be accomplished by manually copying over the contents of the public key file from the client system and pasting them into the **~/.ssh/authorized_keys** file on the SSH server, or you can use the **ssh-copy-id** command: **ssh-copy-id** *user@server*.

ssh_known_hosts

After a connection is established with an SSH server, the SSH client stores the server's unique "fingerprint" key in the user's **.ssh/known_hosts** file:

```
[root@localhost ~]# cat .ssh/known_hosts
|1|trm4BuvRf0HzJ6wusHssj6HcJKg=|EruYJY709DXorogeN5Hdcf6jTCo= ecdsa-
sha2-nistp256AAAAE2VjZHNhLXNoYTItbmlzdHAyNTYAAAAIbmlzdHAyNTYAAABBBG3/
rARemyZrhIuirJtfpfPjUVnph9S1w2NPfEWec/f59V7nAztn5rbcGynNYOdnozdGNNi-
zYAiZ2VEhJ3Y3JcE=
```

Typically the contents of this file should be left undisturbed; however, if the SSH server is reinstalled, then it would have a new "fingerprint" key. This would require all users to remove the entry for the SSH server in the **.ssh/known_hosts** file.

gpg

The GNU Privacy Guard utility, **gpg**, can be used to create public and private encryption keys:

```
[root@localhost ~]# gpg --gen-key
gpg (GnuPG) 1.4.16; Copyright (C) 2013 Free Software Foundation, Inc.
This is free software: you are free to change and redistribute it.
There is NO WARRANTY, to the extent permitted by law.


Please select what kind of key you want:
   (1) RSA and RSA (default)
   (2) DSA and Elgamal
   (3) DSA (sign only)
   (4) RSA (sign only)
Your selection? 1
RSA keys may be between 1024 and 4096 bits long.
What keysize do you want? (2048)
Requested keysize is 2048 bits
Please specify how long the key should be valid.
         0 = key does not expire
      <n>  = key expires in n days
      <n>w = key expires in n weeks
      <n>m = key expires in n months
      <n>y = key expires in n years
Key is valid for? (0)
Key does not expire at all
Is this correct? (y/N) y
You need a user ID to identify your key; the software constructs the
user ID from the Real Name, Comment and Email Address in this form:
    "Heinrich Heine (Der Dichter) <heinrichh@duesseldorf.de>"


Real name: June Jones
Email address: june@jones.com
Comment: Test
You selected this USER-ID:
    "June Jones (Test) <june@jones.com>"


Change (N)ame, (C)omment, (E)mail or (O)kay/(Q)uit? O
You need a Passphrase to protect your secret key.


We need to generate a lot of random bytes. It is a good idea to perform
some other action (type on the keyboard, move the mouse, utilize the
disks) during the prime generation; this gives the random number
```

```
generator a better chance to gain enough entropy.
gpg: key 1946B1F2 marked as ultimately trusted
public and secret key created and signed.

gpg: checking the trustdb
gpg: 3 marginal(s) needed, 1 complete(s) needed, PGP trust model
gpg: depth: 0  valid:   1  signed:   0  trust: 0-, 0q, 0n, 0m, 0f, 1u
pub   2048R/1946B1F2 2017-06-05
      Key fingerprint = 1D6A D774 A540 F98C EBF0  2E93 49D5 711C 1946
B1F2
uid                   June Jones (Test) <june@jones.com>
sub   2048R/FED22A14 2017-06-05
```

NOTE: If you get a message stating "Not enough random bytes available. Please do some other work to give the OS a chance to collect more entropy!", then continue working on your system and it will eventually generate enough random bytes. If you are impatient, try running a system-intensive command such as **sudo find / -type f | xargs grep blahblahblah > /dev/null.**

The result of this command will be a collection of files in the **~/.gnupg** directory that can be used to encrypt data or digitally sign messages.

In order for a user to encrypt data to send to you, that user needs your public key. To send that to a user, first execute the following command to create a public key file:

```
gpg --output pub_key_file  --export 'June Jones'
```

The **--output** option is used to specify the name of the public key file. The **--export** option is used to specify the key you want to send.

After you send the public key, the receiving user imports the key into his GPG database by executing the following command:

```
gpg --import pub_key_file
```

Then the user can encrypt a file using the following command:

```
gpg --encrypt --recipient june@jones.com data.txt
```

After the file has been encrypted, the only way it can be decrypted is on your system with the private key using the **gpg --decrypt** command.

~/.gnupg/

This directory contains a collection of GNU Privacy Guard files. See the "gpg" section in this chapter for more details.

Index

Symbols

& (ampersand), 90
* (asterisk), 81, 103
\ (backslash), 103, 224
` (backtick), 159
[ ] (brackets), 81
^ (caret), 51, 103
$( ) characters, 85
&> characters, 83
$ (dollar sign), 103
! (exclamation point), 51
/ (forward slash), 22, 106–107, 143
< (left arrow), 83
( ) (parentheses), 103
. (period), 103
| (pipe), 83
+ (plus sign), 103
? (question mark), 81, 103, 106–107,
    115, 116
> (right arrow), 83
#! (shebang), 160–161

A

a command (vi), 108
access modes, 133–134
accessibility, 177–180
AccessX, 177
accounts. *See* user accounts
active users, determining, 250–251
addresses (IP)
    CIDR notation, 229–230
    IPv4 versus IPv6, 233–234
    private versus public addresses,
      230–231

alias command, 157
aliases, 157
    aliases file, 222
    email aliases, 222
allocating filesystems, 19
at.allow file, 190–192
alternative boot locations, 25
American Standard Code for Information
    Interchange (ASCII), 207
ampersand (&), 90
anacrontab file, 196–197
apt-cache command, 40–41
apt-get command, 40
aptitude utility, 41
archives, creating, 78
arguments, output as, 85
ASCII (American Standard Code for
    Information Interchange), 207
AT (assistive technology), 178
assumeyes setting (yum.conf file), 46
asterisk (*), 81, 103
at command, 195
atq command, 195
atrm command, 195
audits, 249
authorized_keys file, 269

B

b command (boot loader), 8
background, running processes in, 89–91
backslash (\), 103, 224
backtick (`), 159
bash shell, 52
    .bash_history file, 58
    ~/.bash_login file, 156

F

G

H

To receive your 10% off
Exam Voucher, register
your product at:

www.pearsonitcertification.com/register

and follow the instructions.